For Donald's Great-Grandchildren.

Antony, Matthew, Bryony, Cassia,
Josh & Allegra

Hope, Jack, Luke, Dan, Ned, & Skye

Timothy, Jamie, Lara & Clare

Jessica, Grace, Matthea & Hanya

and Darragh

ISBN# 978-9966-757-4-9-4

Design & Layout by Julia Seth-Smith

Published by Old Africa Books

Printed by English Press

Nairobi, Kenya

DONALD'S WAR

THE DIARY OF A SETTLER IN THE EAST AFRICAN CAMPAIGN

EDITED BY

JULIA SETH-SMITH

&

ANTONY SETH-SMITH

WITH A FORWARD BY

SIR CHARLES MARKHAM

OLD AFRICA BOOKS

"...*a man in Khaki Kit who could handle men a bit.*"

Rudyard Kipling,

TABLE OF CONTENTS

FORWARD

Captain Donald Seth-Smith, MC, could well claim to have been one of the new settler pioneers for he came to Kenya in 1904 when he took up land at Makuyu in partnership with Lord Cranworth, Mervyn Ridley, and the Thompson brothers who were subsequently killed in the Great War.

His son, Antony, has compiled his father's experiences during the First World War from diaries he wrote of the time, adding many valuable photos and numerous press cuttings. Unfortunately, only those covering the period from the start of January 1916 to May 1917 have survived. His 1915 diary covering the Battle of Longido is sadly missing.

The diary has been written from the point of view of an ordinary soldier and officer of the King's African Rifles on the war in British East Africa and the Campaign against General von Lettow in German East Africa.

Antony's book gives a graphic description of the terrible conditions suffered by the huge army facing Von Lettow.

With the war in Flanders and the disaster at Gallipoli, the East African Campaign received little publicity and few people realised the suffering of the British, Indian, South African and Rhodesian troops, not forgetting the thousands of African porters. In many instances lack of water, food and medical attention must have been a horrible nightmare, made worse through the complete lack of experience in fighting a war in thick bush against a brilliant enemy commander, who time and time again escaped to continue his battle against far superior forces.

As a fighting soldier Seth-Smith is more than generous in not blaming the gross inefficiency of the many generals who came and went, and who little deserved such mild censure.

Although his bravery earned him the Military Cross, he suffered greatly from the many terrible hardships and was invalided out of the army in May 1917.

In the years following the end of the Great War, Donald farmed at Njoro and was a most popular man, much loved by all who knew him. He was a great friend of my step-father, Lord Delamere, who died in 1931. That friendship continued with my mother who died twelve year later. I well remember her telling me in one of her very rare letters how much she admired him for his enthusiasm and optimism despite suffering from the ill effects of his war experiences.

I am deeply honoured to have been asked by his son to write this foreword for I am proud to have known a very great man and a true gentleman in every respect. His memory will live forever.

Sir Charles Markham

PREFACE

For many years I have kept stored away in a drawer my father's diaries and letters relating to his early days in what was then British East Africa and now Kenya.

They have been perused and used by various writers over the years as they contain a most interesting glimpse into a period of history rapidly being either forgotten or intentionally misrepresented.

Recently, I pulled out his 1916 diary and started to read. The more I read and thought about the matter-of-fact and unemotional sentences it contains, the more fascinated I became. I discovered too an album with many faded photos relating to the diary's contents and newspaper clippings that further illuminated his personal journal, each one creased and faded by time over some 100 years. Put together, they presented me with a vivid insight into that forgotten campaign from the perspective of someone who was actually there and had experienced it all and who, thank God, lived to tell the tale. He was my father.

My intitial plan was to print the diary exactly as he wrote it. My daugher-in-law, Julia, has taken on the onerous task of turning my idea into reality. In her hands, the diary has become more than just my father's personal account. She has spent the past year reading contemporary accounts and scouring the internet for original source material, and adding comments particularly from my godfather, Lord Cranworth, and from General Von Lettow-Vorbeck whose words and reflections were respected on both sides. Without her invaluable and dedicated support, this account would never have made it to the light of day.

Born on 1st October 1884, my father was already a man of 53 when I was born. He died at the age of 74 when I was still a young man of 21 without the foresight to have asked him about his most interesting and adventurous life. How I regret it now. How much there was to tell of interest to others today, let alone to myself and family.

Now, as I too grow older and have time to reflect on all that has been and what that generation went through and achieved, I feel an immense pride in my father and all that he and his peers stood for.

Those brought up in the strict Victorian manner before the turn of the century were not wont to show their emotions and this comes through in the manuscript. Donald seldom complains or speaks ill of his fellow officers and men, despite the extreme stress of a campaign waged on foot and much of it directed by an incompetent high command.

Only once did I deduce emotion, and then it was unintentional. On the death of a wounded fellow officer he and his men carried back the previous day 11 hours at night, the entry for Thursday November 23rd records simply: "Eckstein died 8.25." The following day's entry: "Funeral of Eckstein 8 am." Both entries were written in small, emotional script without further comment. The day after the funeral, Saturday, November 25th, there is no entry at all. The omission speaks for itself.

In later years he seldom spoke about the campaign except to recall how often, when in the bush on minimal rations, he had wondered how he could conceivably have left in the past the odd egg or sausage on the breakfast sideboard. Remembering how he had witnessed grown men actually fighting over the sugar ration, he was glad that he had never taken sugar in his tea. Two other anecdotes tickled my imagination and have stayed indelibly in my mind. A fellow officer sitting on top of an empty 44-gallon drum had lit a cigarette and casually dropped the match into the empty drum. Presumably there must have been a residue of fuel and probably a lot of gas still trapped as the memory of the resulting flash and the spectacular, though undignified, antics of the now hairless gentleman continued to amuse Donald some 50 years later. Other than his written record, he seldom spoke of his involvement in the many battles and scraps fought with enemy patrols, only once relating a 'contact' when he unexpectedly came round a corner and found a German Officer sitting on a rock 30 yards away in plain view. His only comment: "I missed him clean!"

Donald came to Kenya in 1904 to join his older brother, Martin, who had come out the year before. They were both fine naturalists, keen sportsmen and excellent shots. Donald was elected by his fellow pioneers, together with Freddy Ward, to build Muthaiga Club which they did in 1912. Throughout his time in Kenya he led from in front and was highly respected by his contemporaries.

The 1914 – 18 War saw the whole family participating. Martin fought and died in the German East African Campaign. His younger brother, Kenneth, ran away from Charterhouse at 16, falsifying his age to join the Royal Flying Corp in which he served with distinction. Their only sister, Marjorie, drove ambulances. At the end of the war when Donald was recuperating, his father gave him an inscribed watch which I treasure to this day.

Kenya was at that time England's "Land of Hope and Glory" for which, almost to a man, the settlers fought and some died. Alongside them many extremely brave Africans fought and died too, and they together with the African Carrier Corps, were loyal and invaluable. May their efforts and sacrifices never be forgotten.

Antony Seth-Smith

ACKNOWLEDGEMENTS

Voi is a typical Kenyan town. Once a quiet backwater, it has sprouted into a chaotic urban sprawl accentuated by the noisy commotion of matatus, tinny music and screeching street vendors. In the middle of this hubbub, the small Commonwealth War Graveyard exudes an air of serene dignity and contemplation. It was in this neat little garden, with its lines of regimented grave markers standing sentry in the sisal-dotted gravel that the full magnitude of the futility of the war in East Africa dawned on me. The uniform headstones were a poignant reminder of all those men who fell in this campaign. Lieutenant W.C. Dartnell, awarded the Victoria Cross, is buried here. Here too are the markers for a soldier from the South African Native Labour Corps, a Lieutenant in the 130th Baluchis and one puzzling attribution to 'an unknown camp follower.' But my tears welled up on reading the epitaph "Never forgotten by his sorrowing mother" carved into the headstone of the young Private F.J. Bristow of the Loyal North Lancs. I could envisage her grief at not only losing her son to conflict but also to a strange land, so far away from home.

I have lived most of my life in Kenya and I am embarrassed to admit my ignorance over the Great War in East Africa. It was only when my father-in-law commissioned me to design the layout for his father's war diary and I began to dig into the history that a spark of interest turned into an obsession. It has been an illuminating and occasionally frustrating adventure. A chance e-mail led to my induction into a club of East African Campaign experts who have generously shared their own research and patiently answered my asinine questions. I am indebted to Harry Fecitt, the 'guru' on all things military who has been a mine of information and combed through the archives on my behalf. I am grateful to Anne Samson who was busy with her own deadlines in the lead up to the centenary of the end of the War. She gave up precious time to write encouraging emails, and unasked, sent me Martin Seth-Smith's War file: a mother-lode of information that shed light on his wartime activities. I am also grateful to James Willson, who has been researching the campaign in Tsavo for the past thirty years. His book "Guerillas of Tsavo" has been a valuable source on the early days of the war.

My greatest thanks must go to Tom Lawrence who has been my guide through the quagmire of research. He is an encyclopedia of East African history with files of information on many of the now forgotten personalities of the period. Not only did he share valuable books from his own library, he also arranged for me to join James Willson's guided tour of the Tsavo Battlefields.

Standing in the rubble of the German Blockhouse on Salaita Hill was an enlightening moment. This unprepossessing blip in a sea of scrubby thorn-bush now looks out on twinkling tin roofs bisected by a newly tarmacked road but it is still possible to imagine the noise, the panic and chaos of the battlefield. It was there that I began to comprehend how terrifying the phrase 'fix bayonets' must have been.

This project has been a journey that has led me down some arcane paths. Archivists, including Daniel Reboussin from the Smathers Library in the University of Florida and Rob Petre from Oriel College, have delved into their repositories on my behalf. The National Army Museum in London, in particular the Director and his wife, Justin and Rebecca Maciejewski have been enthusiastic supporters of my efforts. My thanks must also go to Shel and Blake Arensen of Old Africa who have edited, tidied up the faded photos and tweaked the layout for publication.

I have discovered that writing is a very selfish occupation. Absorbed in my research, I have neglected my family and friends. My children, Matthew and Cassia, have been more than tolerant, as has my long-suffering husband, Martin. They have put up with my mental absence and there are not enough adjectives to express my gratitude. My father Douglas, my brother and sister, Dominic and Oily have also been a huge support, as have my friends, especially Nuria Martinez de Velasco and Vittoria Sogno. They have tried hard to keep me sane and drag me back into this century.

This has been a Seth-Smith family endeavour. My sisters-in-law, Tana and Nettie, and Donald's daughter, Anne, have given their whole-hearted endorsement. Sarah Seth-Smith has painstakingly proofread, edited and encouraged me when I floundered in the enormity of the challenge and I am, of course, incredibly grateful to Tony Seth-Smith who began this venture. He generously funded my battlefield safari and the publication of the book.

Once overlooked as an unimportant conflict, the First World War in East Africa is garnering more attention by military historians. Filled with tales of extraordinary exploits, it was the longest campaign of the entire war. However, many of the histories written in the last century were based on inaccurate memoirs and Edward Paice's impeccably researched "Tip and Run" has become my stalwart bible. Where possible I have tried to restrain my research to contemporary accounts and have relied heavily on the writings by Lord Cranworth as he was Donald's close friend and business partner. I have also used Christopher Thornhill's book as one of my main sources as he was, like Martin P. Seth-Smith, in the Intelligence Department.

Most importantly, this is Donald's story and my small additions are intended to illuminate events mentioned in his diary. Any errors and omissions are all mine. The First World War had a lasting impact on everyone in Eastern Africa and I hope the publication of Donald's War will encourage action to preserve East Africa's monuments and battlefields, and also inspire readers to delve into their own family history.

As always, Cranworth deserves the last word:

> "I hope that when the history of the East African Campaign is at length written, justice will be done to the efforts of the inhabitants of Kenya, whether black or white. This was the only part of the British Empire to know invasion, and, partially no doubt from this cause, the response of her white population and the casualties they suffered were in proportion to her numbers greater than any other Colony. Again with regard to the native population: it was not their quarrel nor were they of fighting stock, yet they made overwhelming sacrifices in the common cause. It is not known, I think the truth would be staggering, how many natives in the humble yet essential role of porter laid down their lives. I have always thought that a more generous recognition of their immense services might be forthcoming."

Julia Seth-Smith
Nairobi, September 2018

AFRICA IN 1914

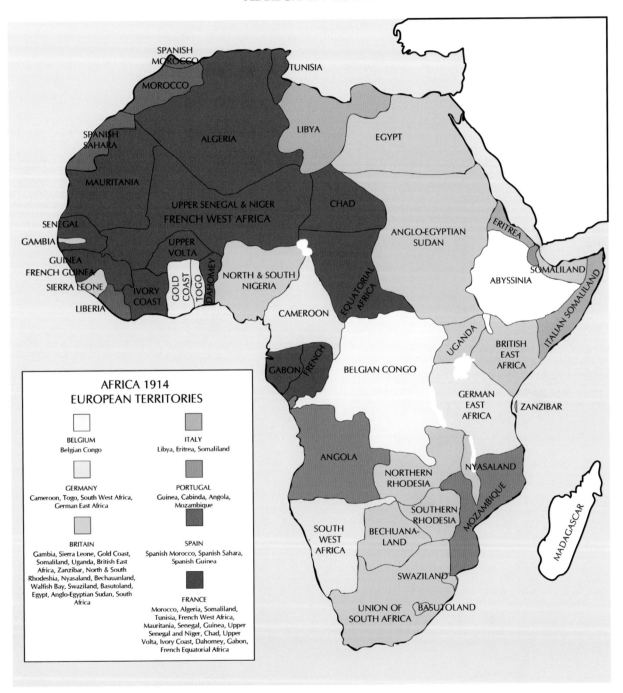

MAP OF BRITISH EAST AFRICA 1906

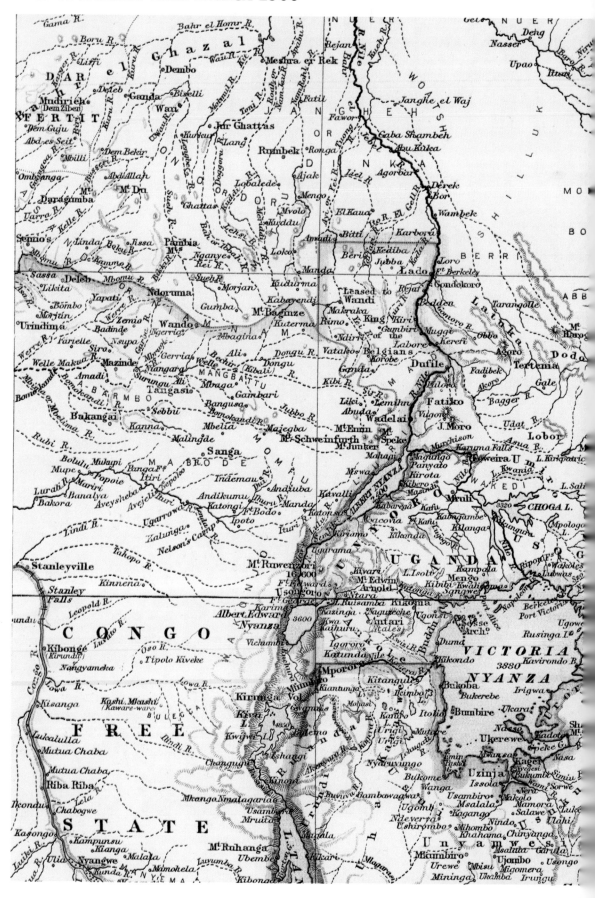

3

Donald on safari with Lord Cranworth

Chapter I
A Farm in Africa

The wild antics of the 'Happy Valley' set have largely overshadowed the contribution of the settlers to the development of East Africa. A plethora of biographies have been written about the more notable characters including 'Cape-to-Cairo' Grogan, Denys Finch-Hatton and the larger-than-life Lord Delamere. History, however, has mainly glossed over those early intrepid pioneers who ranged from farmers, soldiers and Boer trekkers to aristocrats and adventurers. These settlers were seduced by the invitation from the British Colonial Office to lease the vast swathes of seemingly uninhabited land filled with a seemingly limitless supply of wild animals. It was not an altruistic gesture. Saddled with the extortionate cost of building a railway that went through thousands of miles of virgin bush, the British Government was desperate to encourage farmers and traders to create revenue to pay for this 'lunatic line.'

Donald and Martin Seth-Smith were part of that early influx of hunters and emigrants who came to East Africa to make, and sometimes, lose their fortunes. In 1904, whilst still an Oxford undergraduate, Donald made his first trip to British East Africa in the wake of his brother, Martin, a year earlier. So taken was he by those early adventures in the protectorate that he made the decision to leave the family estate, Bolney, in East Sussex and begin a new life in East Africa.

Opposite Page:

Above: "Coming ashore at Mombasa 1906" from Lord Cranworth's book "The Kenya Chronicles." Mombasa Harbour was not deep enough to accommodate large ships and the only way ashore was by small boat.

Below: An early safari from 1909 captioned Dr. Seaman and Giuliras on safari.

This Page:

Above: A young Donald.

Left: Kikuyu Chief 1906.

There is very little official documentation on the Seth-Smiths' activities in East Africa's history. The only references are a rare mention in the odd memoir, a note in the Kenya Gazette or a yellowed, creased newspaper cutting. Just a few personal diaries and letters have survived. However, the family photograph albums supply a treasure trove of information. Stuck haphazardly between snaps of beloved dogs and horses, faded photos of farms, hunting safaris, houses (and the war) are a visual reminder of the brothers' adventures and enterprises.

Correspondence with his father, generally written in a rush to catch the mail[1], is permeated with enthusiasm and with ambitious ideas. The surviving letters are filled with news of ongoing projects (and justification of money spent) and potential investment opportunities. Frequent entreaties for more funds are usually granted by an indulgent and proud parent, including the purchase of the yearned for 'Cooper' steam digging and traction engine (although attempts to bring out the English underkeeper to drive it were unsuccessful.)

Nov 8th 1906.

Nairobi
B.E.A

My dear Dad.
We returned safely from our expedition the night before last having been out just a fortnight & having walked we reckoned about 300 miles altogether – As I know you have a map of the country I will explain to you more or less the way we went – We started from Nairobi & went to the hill marked on the map Donyia Sabuk from there we went to Fort Hall crossing the Athi & Thika rivers & came back down the new road from Fort Hall to Nairobi
It is to Fort Hall that the new railway is talked about (60 miles) & we were told at the Land Office that there was not an available acre between

Top left: Donald on his first safari in 1906.
Bottom left: A copy of the letter describing the safari.

In November 1906, Donald wrote: "The longer one stays here and the more people one meets the more you realise what a really wonderful country this is and what tremendous possibilities there are but you can say it is practically only four years old – it has not yet had a chance, especially as there is no one in the country with any money…"

Having embarked on a series of land purchases in partnership with a fellow Carthusian, Alan Tompson,[2] Donald also made the acquaintance of another recent arrival, Lord Bertram Cranworth. In his rather effusive memoir, "The Kenya Chronicles," Cranworth praises Donald as "well-acquainted with local conditions, and a born farmer and sportsman." In his account of the hunting opportunities, he later describes him as "… another who might well have been the equal of the best of them [hunters] had he cared to undertake the work. That was one of my partners at Makuyu, Donald Seth-Smith, whom as a shooter I have always regarded as, in the best sense of the word, the complete sportsman."

In 1908, Donald bought 25,000 acres beyond Thika with Cranworth, Alan and Ronald Tompson and Cranworth's brother-in-law Mervyn Ridley. Together they formed Sisal Ltd. Donald and Mervyn managed the farm, they named Makuyu after a giant fig tree, As well as planting sisal, they built a processing factory and created an electricity plant. This company now called Kakuzi Ltd. is a successful conglomerate.

Top right: Mervyn Ridley and his dog, Mish.
Bottom left: Martin with one of his hounds.

In 1909 Donald contributed an article to the Oriel College Record with advice for prospective settlers 'with means.' In the article, he extolls the virtues of the climate, the sport, and availability of cheap land and Government grants. He makes recommendations on farming opportunities. whilst omitting mention of the diseases: "malaria, dysentery, typhoid, sunstroke, lion bites and whisky" as described by Cranworth, in his 1911 handbook "A Colony in the Making."

It was not all relentless hard work; English country pursuits were adopted and adapted. Martin, along with Goldfinch and Jim Elkington, had his own pack of hounds and organized a regular jackal hunt. The highlight of Nairobi's social calendar was the bi-annual race meeting when the settlers converged on a Nairobi to meet friends, exchange news and enjoy themselves. And of course there were the hunting trips. Donald, occasionally together with Martin, went out on safari. Both brothers were brilliant shots and avid naturalists.

Opposite Page
Above: Donald and unknown (possibly Mervyn Ridley) loading a cart.
Below: Martin standing outside his house - perhaps Ruaraka Hall - surrounded by his hounds.
On the back of photo the caption reads: "my grass hut soon to be demolished as there are as many fleas and jiggers inside as there are pieces of grass in the roof."
This page: "Inspanning the oxen" - a safari on the Uasin Gishu Plateau.

Top left: Donald, D. Fawcus and Mervyn Ridley on the verandah at Makuyu.

Above from left to right: Bernard Cazenove, J. Harvey, H.K. Wood, Frank Allsopp and Donald Seth-Smith, 1910.

Left: Makuyu is the setting for many photos of this period. A pride of lions were spotted sitting under an old fig tree. It was decided that, if it was good enough for the lions, it was good enough for a house site. A solid house was built for Lady Cranworth who was also responsible for laying out the garden.

THE LEADER OF BRITISH EAST

AN M. P. ON SAFARI.

Two Rare Animals.

Mr. David Davies, M.P. (Montgomeryshire) and Mrs. Davies, have been on safari to the west of Kenia, striking through Fort Hall, and Nyeri to the Guaso Nyiro district. They were accompanied by Dr. Welsh, and were under the capable guidance of Mr. M. P. Seth-Smith. Having secured their outfit from the firm Messrs. Newland, Tarlton and Co., the party set off in January with a body of about 150 Kikuyu porters. The caravan consisted of nearly two hundred persons. Mr. Davies and Dr. Welsh proved to be excellent shots and good sportsmen. They secured a very fair mixed bag, including rhino, oryx, eland, leopard and buffalo. There were two strange animals secured on the journey, namely a red, fox-coloured monkey and a fennec fox The former is a species of colobus monkey, but differs in its habits considerably, and it not often seen out of the Uasin Gishu. The fennec fox belongs to Somaliland and has only recently been discovered south of the Equator. Four fine buffalo were shot on the Athanga Hills near the end of the trip. The party returned to Nairobi on Thursday, March 2nd, the trip being somewhat curtailed by the indisposition of one of the party.

To make their bag complete, these sportsmen are proceeding to Kapiti Plains, where they hope to secure a lion, and on return they will go after Jacksonii and topi, proceeding thence to the Victoria Nyanza.

Martin is rarely mentioned. There is reference to his brief involvement in a granary and timber yard, but it seems that he preferred to pursue sporting interests. Martin's only surviving diary is a detailed account of his trip to the Uasin Gishu in 1908. Two newspaper cuttings, from 1911, carefully preserved by the family back in England, describe Martin as the professional hunter and his adventures hunting elephant beyond Baringo. In the same year records show that he joined the Game Department.[3]

While Donald and Martin were finding their feet in British East Africa, their cousin, Leslie, had arrived in the adjacent protectorate. Initially employed as surveyor, he settled in Uganda around 1906 and from there went on to become a planter. In July 1912, when Donald and Martin's father (also called Martin) made his anticipated visit to East Africa, they travelled up to Uganda to visit Leslie. His uncle described him in his diary as "said to be most popular man in Uganda."[5]

Opposite page, clockwise from the top: Martin (far right) on Safari.

Right: Donald's great friend Freddie Ward, who built Muthaiga Club.

Far left: The press cutting describing Martin as a Professional Hunter.

This page, above: Martin's gunbearer Ndolo and Juma on the road to Baringo, 1908.

Below: Using an ox team to plough up the land.

15

With the exception of the photograph albums, there is a vacuum for the years 1911 to 1913. Donald is only mentioned in association with the founding of the Muthaiga Club. Later infamous as the setting for the parties of the 'Happy Valley' set, the Club was created as an exclusive sanctuary for select settlers following the long antipathy with Colonial officials (who considered the existing Nairobi Club as their domain)[5]. The building was funded by the fabulously wealthy Major Archie Morrison. Visiting Kenya for a hunting safari, he was wooed by Freddie Ward as a potential investor for the country. On a whistle-stop tour of Nairobi, Morrison decided that a farm on the outskirts was the ideal place for a residential development with the proviso that a club was built. Freddie was responsible for the building of the club and became the first secretary. Morrison never returned to see his investment.

The Muthaiga Club, painted a distinctive pink, employed a Head Chef from the Bombay Yacht Club, boasted the best wine cellar in Africa, and had a shop which in one member's opinion was "an Apsrey in miniature."[6]

On the 31st January 1913, fourteen members (there is no record of whether Donald was there), sat down for the first dinner, complete with trimmings, crackers, hats and a band.

Opposite page: Donald is pictured with the hunters, Philip Percival and Jack Lucy in 1914.
(courtesy of the Smathers Library, University of Florida)

Above: Nairobi in 1913.

Left: A photo in Martin's Photograph Album showing the back of The Norfolk Hotel.

Chapter II
The German Lion

I n 1914, as the Goan waiters cleaned up the debris from the Muthaiga Club's inaugural dinner, the SS Admiral from the Deutsche Ost-Afrika Line was well on her way to Mombasa. On board were two passengers who would put their own stamp on the history of East Africa. One was a young Dane, Karen Dinesen, who was to become the most famous chronicler of the Kenya colony. The other was Paul von Lettow-Vorbeck, a Prussian Junker[1] in the German Army. They became friends on board and perhaps, as has been intimated (and gossiped about in society of the time), indulged in a romance. The SS Admiral docked in Mombasa on 13th January 1914 where they parted ways: Karen to marry her fiancé Baron Bror Blixen, Von Lettow-Vorbeck to continue his journey on to Dar-es-Salaam in German East Africa. However, they planned to meet up once more for a safari before the year was out. Despite the gurgles of discontent in the Europe they left behind, neither could imagine that by August 1914, they would be on opposing sides.

Von Lettow was on his way to take command of the *Schutztruppe* or defence forces in German East Africa. With his customary thoroughness, he had prepared himself well in advance by studying the maps of the territory and learning Swahili. No sooner had he arrived in Dar-es-Salaam and presented his credentials to Governor Schnee, than he literally got on his bicycle to make a tour of all the *Schutztruppe* detachments. For six months, he travelled the length and breadth of the colony inspecting the terrain, munitions and soldiers. Sleeping under the stars, he delighted in the landscape, the wildlife and the people. He was full of praise for the local Africans and their inventiveness. He spent nights in the many Missions scattered across the country and drank Moselle with the German settlers in their comfortable plantation houses.

That Paul Emil von Lettow-Vorbeck was a soldier was unsurprising. Four generations of his family had served in the military. His father was a General who had fought in the Franco-Prussian war. There was no discussion about the young Paul's future and his education prepared him for a traditional Prussian army career, first in the cadets corps and then the military academy at Kassel.

It was not until 1900, at the age of thirty, when von Lettow experienced his first battle in the Boxer Rebellion. He had gone out to China as a staff officer to the German contingent of the

Above: Von Lettow-Vorbeck, 1913.
(courtesy of the Bundesarchiv)

allied forces where, unlike many staff officers, he had volunteered to fight. He observed, with some prescience, that the British troops were very competent but "abysmally" led by commanders who would "delay, delay, delay."

His next action was in German South West Africa to put down the Herero-Hottentot Rebellions. This was a war that did not adhere to the military rulebooks. It was bloody guerilla fighting in a dust-bowl that was waterless and disease-infested. Even von Lettow did not escape unscathed, receiving a chest wound and temporarily losing the use of his eye in a bungled ambush.[2]

But it was from the Hottentots, those 'half-naked warriors' who had trounced the modern German military, that von Lettow learnt the valuable skills that would stand him in good stead in his engagement with the Allies. Travelling light, deploying small units, living off the country, and using lightning attacks on the enemy were just some of the lessons learned, but the most important was that of using a local fighting force, that was versed in bushcraft, used to living off an inhospitable terrain and less susceptible to disease.

Germany had initially controlled its young colony with the *kiboko* (a hippo-hide whip) and the tales of cruelty inflicted on the Africans who dared resist their colonisers make for uncomfortable reading. However, by 1914, under the administration of Governor Schnee and his predecessor, German East Africa was considered an enlightened, modern protectorate with roads, hospitals and a research centre focusing on the study of tropical disease. Even the *Schutztruppe* were a liberal concept with the main force made up of African NCOs under a handful of white German commanders.

Had von Lettow some notion of the impending outbreak of hostilities or was he just a very conscientious *Oberleutnant*? Whilst the Balkan wars had put Europe on an uneasy footing, would anyone have known that far in advance that the assassination on June 28th of the Austrian Archduke Ferdinand and his wife triggered a series of events that led to England and Germany declaring war on each other?

General Count von Lettow-Vorbeck with colleagues on the veranda.
(courtesy of the Imperial War Museum)

He gives no hint in his memoir "Reminiscences of East Africa", except to mention that in June 1914, he had heard that "foreign Arabs and Swahili were appearing in the country, and telling people that the Germans would soon be going and the English would take possession of the land." It was not until the beginning of August that he received news via heliograph and telegram that the Kaiser had ordered mobilization of men. Von Lettow raced back to Dar-es-Salaam to receive further orders.

At the beginning of August, Dar-es-Salaam hosted a grand exhibition. Ostensibly conceived to commemorate the opening of the railway, it was a display of German progress and achievements in agriculture and industry. A festival air permeated the seaside capital, and the streets were full of settlers and visitors who had travelled from Germany for the event. Part of the attraction was the state-of-the-art three-funnelled light cruiser, The Konigsberg, armed with her 4.1" armour-piercing guns, moored in the port. Garlanded with colourful bunting, she took guests on excursions out to sea to show off her power.

As soon as The Konigsberg's commander, Max Loof, was informed of the escalation in hostilities, he made preparations to leave. He was well aware that the British were the superior navy in the Indian Ocean and would converge on Dar-es-Salaam to blockade the port. On 31st July, the Konigsberg[3] slipped anchor and headed out to the open seas, outrunning the aged British HMS Pegasus and Astraea.

Not all German officials were spoiling for a scrap. Governor Schnee believed (as did his British counterpart, Governor Belfield) that the colony had no obligation to engage in war. The Congo Treaty of 1885 intimated that a 'possession' could remain neutral in the event of a conflict between European 'owners'. It was a mutual concern that "the inviolability of the white man must be maintained if a few hundred white men were to continue governing many thousands of blacks in safety"[4] and this 'apple-cart' would be upset if the Africans saw white men fight each other. Or the unthinkable: black men legitimately killing Europeans.

Von Lettow's memoir mildly recounts the disagreement between himself and Schnee but from other accounts it was an all-out fight resulting in von Lettow's insubordination. He ignored the Governor's orders and began preparations to mobilise his *askaris*, reservists and police force. Meanwhile, unbeknownst to von Lettow, Schnee had been negotiating a truce for Dar-es-Salaam. Schnee has been portrayed as a bungling pacifist, but he was a pragmatic administrator with a brilliant legal brain. It made sense to maintain open ports on the German East African coastline rather than be attacked by the British navy.

The ink was barely dry on the declaration of war when three days later, on the 8th August, the

HMS Astraea bombarded the wireless masts behind Government House.[5] She was unable to enter Dar-es-Salaam port due to the Germans having scuttled one of their ships, the Mowe, at the entrance. This was the first recorded attack on Germany in the First World War. With the destruction of the radio masts, German East Africa was mainly cut off from the 'Fatherland'. Von Lettow was issued with an executive order of command. He was now in charge of war preparations.

On the 13th August, the British protectorate found itself under attack when the small border town of Taveta was invaded and occupied by a force of 300 German reservists under the command of Captain Tom von Prince[6] and Captain Albrecht Hering. Von Lettow had made his first move.

Throughout the rest of the war, von Lettow was to prove himself a master in this military chess game. Well aware that he could not match the British in man power or resources, his strategy was to draw troops away from the main theatre of war in Europe. He also set the pace of the war, dictating where the skirmishes would be fought and on his terms. By capturing Taveta, situated between the Pare Mountains and Mount Kilimanjaro, he had effectively sealed off the corridor into German East Africa.

The German Camp in Taveta, 1914.

(courtesy of the Bundesarchiv)

"A Vita Between the Wazungu"

British East Africa at War

Chapter III
War

News of the impending war with Germany spread like wildfire. The European population[1] were filled with patriotic fervour. They left their homes in their droves and congregated in Nairobi. For many of them, leaving their struggling farms in the hands of a long-suffering wife or local headman was a foolhardy gesture. After war was officially declared on 5th August, Nairobi teemed with men sporting bandoleers and brandishing whatever firearm they could muster from dainty pistols, big colt revolvers to sporting rifles and elephant guns. They cobbled together their own individual uniforms from what they had. Battered double *terai* hats decorated with strips of leopard skin, flannel khaki shirts and whatever breeches they had to hand were the popular choices[2].

In conjunction with the proclamation of war, the Governor, Sir Henry Belfield, had also instated Martial law. Not that this stopped the bars from staying open all day and all night. A tented city popped up at the racecourse, reminiscent of the original 'Tentfontein' of the early Nairobi. As the weeks dragged on, more and more men milled around the bars, shops and street corners. The local government had made no provision for the volunteers and a recruitment centre had to be hastily organized in Nairobi House. There must have been a festive atmosphere. A few men, including Grogan, were not so gung-ho but the majority were euphoric and excited.

As Christopher Thornhill, who had only heard about the war from an Indian shopkeeper way out in the bush, succinctly put it, "I felt I couldn't breathe until I had joined something."

The rumour mill was in full swing. Spies, planes and even zeppelins[3] were spotted and nicely summed up by the little ditty

> I thought I saw an aeroplane
> Upon the Athi Plains
> I looked again,
> And saw it was a Kavirondo crane.

Belfield, like Schnee, had no appetite for war and even when the settlers organized themselves into units, including one named after himself and another for his daughter, Monica, he refused to entertain the idea of a volunteer army. In hindsight, it seems strange: British East Africa's limited defence force, the King's African Rifles, was made up of only three battalions of which only one 3/K.A.R. was based in British East Africa. The other battalions, the 1/K.A.R. and 4/K.A.R. operated out of Nyasaland (modern day Malawi) and Uganda. This professional *Askari* army, together with the East African Mounted Rifles, was the only available fighting force in those early months of the war. Whilst undisciplined and indifferent to army regulations, the first settler volunteers were comprised of good horsemen and excellent shots with an in-depth knowledge of the land and language. They certainly did not deserve the comment made by one Indian Army Officer that they were "great fellows in the bar… but they make one quite nervous fighting."

Eventually, after spending nervous nights under canvas listening to the hysterical giggles of nearby hyena, some units of the nascent East Africa Mounted Rifles were given their movement orders. A young Elspeth Huxley recalled seeing the first squadron, a motley collection riding an assortment of badly behaved mounts, parade past Governor Belfield before cantering down to the railway station.

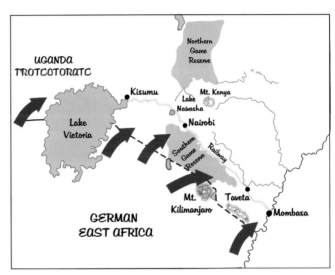

Map showing 1914 proposed German attack routes into British East Africa.

In Mombasa, no time was wasted in organizing a volunteer home guard. The coastal strip was unprotected and the only heavy weaponry available were the 19th century Portuguese muzzle-loading cannon, last used to defend a besieged Fort Jesus from the invading Arabs. Under the command of a former Navy Commander, these were wheeled into position and some rudimentary mines manufactured to protect the harbour. The Mombasa townspeople had every right to be concerned. In September 1914, the *Schutztruppe* columns were getting dangerously close to Mombasa. Winding their way up the South Coast, they were kept at bay by Wavell's Arab Rifles and later the 1/K.A.R. The German threat was omnipresent and it was not until November that the detachments were sent to reinforce Gazi on the coast and Mweli Mdogo beyond the Shimba Hills.

Governor Sir Henry Belfield.

Volunteers continued to flock into Nairobi. A plan of potential enemy attack routes had been formulated and it was decided that the East African Mounted Rifles be used to patrol the long Anglo-German border, most of which was made up of the Southern Game Reserve, as well as the parts of the railway which were deemed most vulnerable.

Christopher Thornhill's account of the war, serving first in the East African Mounted Rifles and later in the Intelligence Department, reads like a 'Boys Own' manual. He vividly describes his unit, Bowker's Horse, made up of young men fresh from their Nairobi desks who never been in the bush let alone ridden a horse or mule before. Barely able to walk from hours spent in the saddle, they learnt to cope with an austere diet of antelope meat and water (often drunk from leech-infested waterholes).

Describing sentry duty, Thornhill conjures up a spirit of Africa that resonates with anyone who has spent a night on safari: "In place of the tense darkness and unknown beyond, a fairyland spectacle lay before us. Gleaming in the silvery moonlight the valleys were covered in mist the hillocks were islands set in seas of opalescent silver."

While von Lettow concentrated his efforts in the North of German East Africa, his Commanders, acting on their own initiative, were attempting to invade Nyasaland and Northern Rhodesia. Under the command of Wahle, the Germans besieged Abercorn, which was subsequently relieved when reinforcements arrived and Wahle retreated back over the border. The Germans also attacked Lukuga in the Congo thereby negating the neutrality clause enshrined in the 1885 Congo Treaty; the Belgians retaliated. Meanwhile, the Germans had gathered in force in Moshi near Kilimanjaro where they made constant lightning strikes on the tracks of the Uganda Railway.

The War Office, no doubt swamped with mobilisation and logistics for the Western Front, had left the military planning in the hands of the Colonial and India Offices. 10,000 imperial troops from India, together with the regiment of Royal North Lancs, were crammed into transports destined for East Africa.

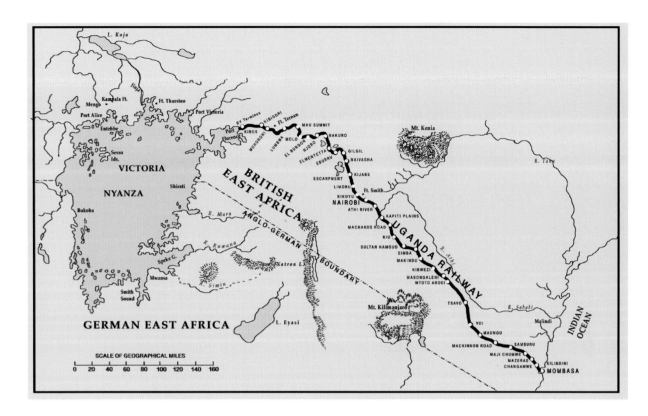

An ambitious plan had been hatched to rout out the Germans in a two-pronged attack from the Longido Line towards Kilimanjaro commanded by Brigadier General Stewart and from the port of Tanga in the South under the commands of Brigadier General Tighe and Brigadier General Wapshare. In overall command was Major General Aitken.

The three-day battle of Tanga, that commenced on the 2nd November, turned into a bloody debacle that culminated in the heavily demoralized Indian Expeditionary 'B' Force retreating to their boats. They left the Germans with the gift of eight machine guns, half a million rounds of ammunition, telephone equipment, uniforms and blankets. British casualties would be tallied at 817. The Germans lost 125 men. Aitken was quietly dismissed. Apart from a few lines in The Leader, the local British East African newspaper, reports of the failed battle were muzzled in the British press and not made public until long after the war ended.

Whilst the Germans and their *askaris* in particular, were ecstatic at having routed the 'Indian she-goats,'[5] British fighting morale was at an all time low. Von Lettow later described Tanga as the "birthday of our soldierly spirit in our troops."

Opposite Page: Vasco da Gama Street near Fort Jesus in Mombasa.
Above: A map of the Uganda Railway Line in 1914.

The Battle of Tanga was not the only humiliation for the British. At the beginning of November the Expeditionary 'C' Force, under the command of Stewart, arrived at Mount Longido, north-west of Kilimanjaro. Unlike at Tanga, where the British Imperial Army had been the only troops in the Expeditionary 'B' Force, Stewart's army also included the East African Mounted Rifles and the K.A.R. who had been patrolling the Anglo-German border. A clash between the enemies in the mist-covered mountain of Longido resulted in failure.

Piecing together Donald and Martin's early wartime involvement has been like assembling a jumble of missing jigsaw pieces; the military records are scant. However, they reveal that Martin joined the Intelligence Department on 5th August 1914. Lord Delamere was responsible for creating the Intelligence Department, and as well using his good connections with the Masai (who were unwilling to fight but made excellent spies) he also recruited the Game Department. Wardens including Richard Woosnam and Geroge Goldfinch enlisted at the same time as Martin. Ewart Grogan was also noted down in the records as a member of the I.D.

Donald joined the Supply Corps in November 1914 together with Grogan's brother, Quentin. His responsibility was getting teams of ox-wagon laden with supplies across to the army camps strategically based in Kedongai and Bissel. In 1915, the war became a simmering set of skirmishes. That January, Belfield made a speech urging the settlers to return to their farms and bring in the harvest. Many heeded his advice. Some such as Woosnam and the Tompson cousins left

East Africa for the Western Front. Woosnam was killed in Gallipoli a few months later and the Tompsons both lost their lives in France.

Donald returned to farming. The only surviving letter from this period[6] is concerned with his business affairs. However, he writes, "We may have labour troubles – sisal market troubles – shipping troubles or be beaten by the Germans and so be broken to the world but at the moment we are sitting fairly safely on the edge of a volcano." In his usual haste to catch the mail, he finishes, "I must stop now… I am also going to pay another call to Headquarters Staff and see if there is any news as I do so want to get back and do another 'bit.'"

Above: Donald's photograph of an Ox team on the way to Kedongai.

Opposite: The K.A.R. Mess in 1914. An invitation to an evening at the Mess was eagerly anticipated by many a settler.

On 7th September 1915, 1,500 settlers, civil servants and a small group of Indians gathered in the Theatre Royal to hear Grogan deliver a passionate patriotic speech calling for support of the war. The response was so deafening that Mr Radley, the manager of the Theatre, was concerned that the roof might cave in. Having lambasted both settlers and civil servants for dodging the war effort, Grogan called for conscription. He also urged provincial officers to take on the farms of absent farmers and for the women (with the accolade "if you want anything well done...") to do their part. The settlers voted in favour and a week later Belfield conceded to Grogan's demands. A war council was established and the Protectorate became the first British territory to pass a law for conscription.

1915 ended on a more positive note than how it had started. There was news of the imminent arrival of the well-respected General Smith-Dorrien. Troops were being deployed from the Western Front along with the shipping of armaments and mechanised transport. This was no longer a half-hearted campaign. The new army was a compendium of nationalities from the Indians in the Imperial Force, The Rhodesians, South Africans (including Cape Coloured), and later forces from Nigeria, Gold Coast and as far away as the West Indies.

Donald got his wish to do 'his bit' and was enlisted in Logan's Battery. He started writing a diary. Starting with his entrainment to the new army camp in the heart of the waterless and thorn-scrub Tsavo bush, he kept meticulous notes of the day-to-day events. His diary is a fascinating historical document that covers the period January 1916 to May 1917. It covers the events leading up to the battles of Salaita Hill and Latema Nek and the subsequent pushing out of the Germans out of British East Africa deep into Southern Tanganyika.

(Note: the diary which follows has been transcribed straight from the original including Donald's phonetic spelling: Salaita is known as Solyta, Lake Jipe is known as Jippe and he calls the Njoro Drift, Langoro Drift. Van Deventer is also called Van Der Wenter.)

GEORGE HAMMOND GOLDFINCH

George Goldfinch, distinguished by his long bushy beard, is not mentioned in the diary. However, he pops up in Donald's father's diary during his grand tour of East Africa in 1912. His father cryptically wrote of Goldfinch "… should think him unique in B.E.A. or anywhere else". He was clearly a great friend of Martin's: not only were they in the Game Department together, he was named as one of the executors of Martin's estate, together with Blayney Percival. Martin and Goldfinch shared a passion for hunting with hounds and Goldfinch was the second master of the Masara Hounds.

Goldfinch arrived from South Africa in 1904. It seems he fought in the Boer War and resigned his commission to take up a position as stock inspector in the Protectorate. He was later employed as the Game Ranger for the Naivasha Province. In 1912 he was the officer in charge of the controversial moving of the Maasai from Laikipia to the Southern Game Reserve. It is thought that he was the 'mole' that shared valuable information with those against the translocation. He was briefly enlisted in the Intelligence Department at the beginning of the war, but in 1915 returned to the Game Department as the only Game Warden for the duration of the war.

Philip Percival describes Goldfinch in 1905 when he was staying with Percival's brother, Blayney, in Parklands as a "dear old gentleman of independent means." In 1906, whilst hunting on the Athi Plains with George Lucas, a lion sprang up out of the long grass and attacked Goldfinch, wounding him in the thigh before turning on Lucas who was mauled in the face and arm. Goldfinch managed to shoot the lion and get both of them to safety. Lucas died from his wounds in Nairobi Hospital a week later. Goldfinch survived. Retold by many hunters of the period, the story became a cautionary tale on the cunning and ferocity of the East African lions.

He appears to have kept up a lively correspondence on a number of issues - ranging from his views on the missionaries in East Africa to notes on the African crested rat and a colour anomaly in a specimen of Grant's zebra. George Goldfinch died in Nyeri in 1926

Photographs of George Goldfinch from Martin's album.

THE SETTLERS AT WAR

It must have been chaos when the volunteers descended on Nairobi in August 1914 clamouring for a 'scrap'. A recruitment office was hastily set up in Grogan's building, Nairobi House, but there were no uniforms or weapons. The Settlers, used to being self-sufficient, marshalled themselves into some sort of order and set up irregular companies. Russell Bowker Douglas, a hoary old settler, arrived in town wearing a cap fashioned from a snarling leopard head. He started Bowker's Horse (they were later nicknamed 'Bowker's Foot' after they had their horses rustled from them at Longido) and positions in his unit were coveted. Monica's Own, named in honour of Governor Belfield's daughter, fancied themselves as Lancers, had iron-tipped bamboo lances rustled up in the railway workshop complete with red and white pennants. Luckily the lances were short-lived. They were later known as the corps that fought first and trained later.

The South African Boers, who apparently carried on to Nairobi, straight from their own war council in the Uasin Gishu plateau, formed their own corps. Wessel's, Arnoldi's and Ross's Scouts were also formed. Settlers such as Denys Finch Hatton, joined Berkeley Cole's Somali Scouts, a unit made up of Somali volunteers. As the war preparations became more organized, the irregular companies were amalgamated under the East African Mounted Rifles. By the end of August some 400 volunteers had signed up to fight. Some form of discipline and training was instilled but the settlers found it difficult to conform to an army regime. As Elspeth Huxley wrote:

"A camp was formed on the racecourse but most of the troopers lived either in one of the hotels, in the recently opened country club, with Nairobi friends or even at Government House.

'Where are troopers Ridley and Thompson?' enquired the second-in-command who was inspecting the camp one evening, observing that two of the sentries were missing. 'Oh, they're dining at Government House,' the sergeant replied, 'but H.E.'s promised to send them home early in his car.'"

During the first two months of the war, the E.A.M.R. and K.A.R. were the only forces available and managed to prevent further German incursions in to British East Africa. Based between Kajiado and Namanga, at Il Bissel, and Kedongai, the E.A.M.R. patrolled the lengthy border between German and British East Africa, flushing out German raiding parties. Initially there was no support unit until the later formation of the supply corps. Alongside Grogan's brother Quentin and Bror Blixen, Donald managed the ox teams carting supplies, water and the sick.

In November 1914, the E.A.M.R. were part of the advance on Longido. Despite their knowledge and experience gleaned from months in the saddle reconnoitring the area, army hierarchy dictated that senority in rank put the raw Indian officers in charge. The poorly planned battle was a disaster that resulted in the loss of many settler lives.

Lord Cranworth, having joined the Norfolk Yeomanry at the outbreak of war, sailed out with Colonel Kitchener (elder brother of Lord Kitchener) at the beginning of 1915 to advise on the possible formation of a larger African force. On finishing his report he joined forces with Berkeley Cole's Somali Scouts. In "Kenya Chronicles" Cranworth describes how they painted stripes on the ponies with iodine. He recalls this period as being pleasant and uneventful enlivened by sightings of herds of ivory-laden elephant and prides of lions. One piece of excitement was the rumour of a German lady, 'Bibi Sacharani,' who was purported to seek revenge for the death of her husband by killing and mutilating white soldiers. Patrols were reminded to "Look out for the Bibi!"

On July 15th 1915, Cole's Scouts proved themselves an effective force in the battle of Mbuyuni, ordered by General Malleson. When the well-entrenched German machine guns fired on the main British column, killing the Commanding Officer of the 29th Punjabis, Cole's Scouts retaliated with their own machine gun, causing many casualties. Cranworth relates, how, in the early stages of the battle, "I was never more frightened in my life." He gives a chilling account of his hat being shot off, a close encounter with a German *askari* and killing three German officers.

The rest of 1915 saw the British forces unwillingly engaged in a slow bush war of attrition. Most of the E.A.M.R. trickled away back home and units such as Cole's Scouts were disbanded. When the settlers returned to war at the beginning of 1916, they were re-assigned to battalions in the reinforced allied army.

At its zenith, the E.A.M.R. had six squadrons, a machine gun section and a section of signallers. By 1917 it simply shrank to nothing. However, their capability and bravery was acknowledged. As Captain Wilson noted in his History of the E.A.M.R: "The record of the East African Mounted Rifles must be almost unequalled as regards the proportion of men who received commissions from the ranks."

Opposite page: A rare photograph of the East African Mounted Rifles.
(courtesy of the National Army Museum)

This page: A photo of Russell Bowker Douglas in his leopard cap from Newland & Tarlton's 1917 Handbook, Farming & Planting in East Africa.

The ox wagons used to transport supplies.

Kedongai Camp.

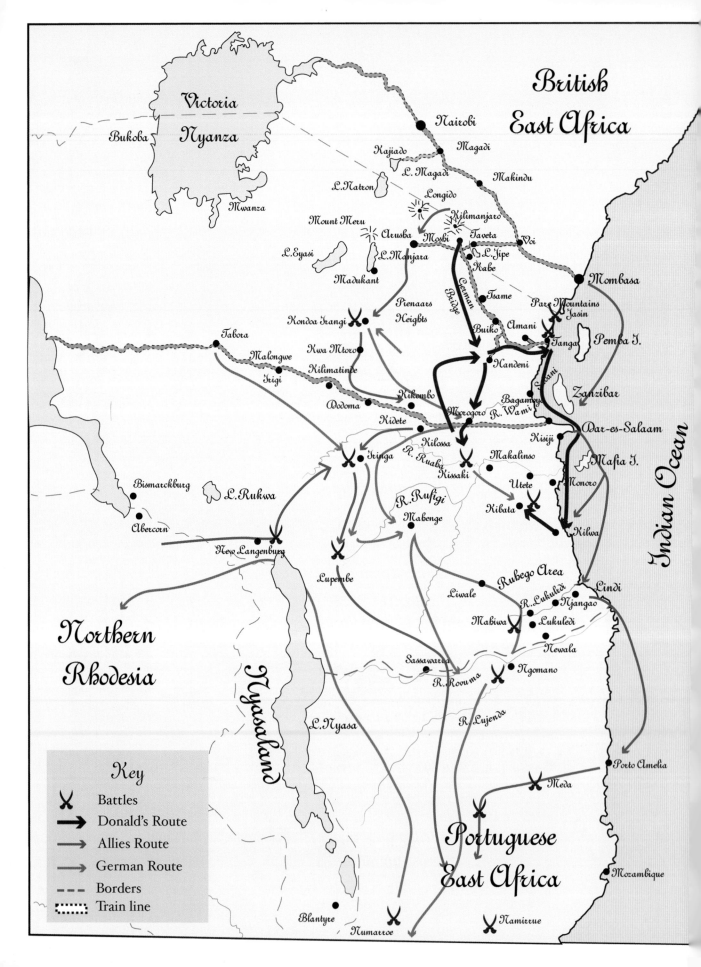

THE DIARY OF
CAPTAIN DONALD SETH-SMITH M.C.

"Tipperary Mbali Sana Sana"
The King's African Rifles marching song

JANUARY 1916

Saturday, January 1st

In camp at Maktau on Serengeti plains 40 miles from Voi – flat waterless country – a few miles further on country undulated in long ridges, the tops of which are covered with dense wait-a-bit thorn scrub, the lower bits being clearer with big mimosa trees and enormous baobabs, most of which have pegs for ladders made by the Germans for observation purposes. Voi on the Uganda Railway to Taveta, our boundary Government Post on the German border is about 78 miles and a good road runs all the way. The railway was commenced six months after war broke out for military purposes only as Taveta is held by the Germans and they have also three or four other camps between Maktau and Taveta so we have 40 miles of British East Africa (BEA) to push the Huns out of before we get to German East Africa (GEA).

Sunday, January 2nd

Quiet day in camp.

Monday, January 3rd

Brigade training which means our battery, No 1 Light (2 naval 12-pounders), also Calcutta Battery (6 12-pounders), and 6 10-pounder Mountain Battery guns go out a few miles in the bush and practice getting into position etc.

Our Battery, which is drawn by 7 Hupp motors are naval guns. 2 cars draw guns, 2 draw limbers , 2 for ammunition, and 1 for spares and mechanics etc.

Our Major, Logan by name, has applied for heavier cars but wishes to keep us on as drivers as he has now been training us for 4 months semaphore, getting guns into position, carrying up ammunition etc.

Tuesday, January 4th

Eckstein and I are given 48 hours leave in Nairobi although it will take us 22 hours train journey to get there.

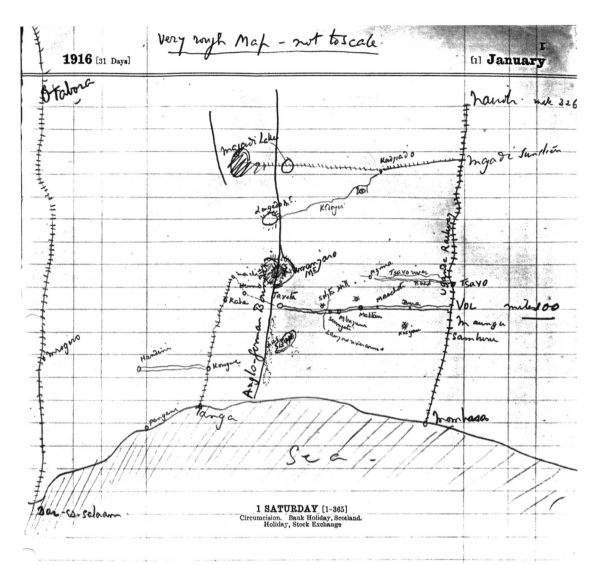

1 SATURDAY [1-365]
Circumcision.   Bank Holiday, Scotland.
Holiday, Stock Exchange

In Camp at Maktau on Serengeti plains 40 miles
from Voi . flat waterless country ~~with no water~~
- a few miles further on country undulates in long
ridges the tops of which are covered with
dense wait-a-bit thorn scrub - the lower
slopes being clearer with big mimosa trees
and enormous baobab trees - most of which
have pegs in for ladders - made by the
germans for observation purposes - Voi on
the Uganda Railway to Taveta our boundary
government Post on the german border is about
75 miles & a good road runs all the way - The
railway was commenced 6 months after war broke

Wednesday & Thursday, January 5th & 6th

In Nairobi.

Friday, January 7th

Left Nairobi 10.45. Train delayed on journey owing to the Op. train having had to stop to pick up bombs found on the line.

Saturday, January 8th

Arrived back in Maktau. Found tent full of dust as strong winds have been blowing the last day or two and the place is full of dust. Two aeroplanes went out this morning and dropped bombs on Serengeti and Taveta camps.

We hear that Jones of the Infantry Division (I.D.) has been killed down by Samburu.

Sunday, January 9th

Quiet day in camp.

Monday, January 10th

The two 4-inch naval guns (recovered from Pegasus) have firing practice. Baluchis left camp in a hurry in the afternoon for Samburu where a small German force has been seen advancing towards the line. They arrived late we heard afterwards. The Arab Scouts drove off the Germans but lost rather heavily and Wavell was killed.

Tuesday, January 11th

Gun practice.

Wednesday, January 12th

Another aeroplane smashed up (Caudron). It rose 25 feet, side stepped, and crashed down. Pilot Brown was unhurt.

Scrap down the line near Maungu. Mountain Battery did good work and was supposed to have killed about 2 officers and 40 men.

AIR VICE-MARSHALL SIR LESLIE OSWALD BROWN
K.B.E., O.B.E., C.B., D.S.C. AND BAR, D.F.C.

Research reveals that Pilot Brown went on to have a distinguished career in the Royal Airforce. After flying in East Africa (where he was awarded the D.S.C), he stayed in the newly-formed RAF and served with distinction in the Second World War.

One charming story associated with Brown was recorded by the photographer, Cherry Kearton. Brown had a pet baboon that was so attached to him it would watch as he flew reconnaissance missions, staying patiently on the airfield to watch the aircraft leave. It seemed to know which plane Brown was flying as it would start squealing with excitement at the sound of his return. On one mission the Caudron he was flying crashed (perhaps the one mentioned by Donald). The baboon saved Brown's life. Its agitation alerted Kearton and a search party was sent out. He had been brought down close to enemy lines and rescued by a scouting patrol.

Thursday, January 13th

Nothing

Friday, January 14th

Arrival of General Malleson and staff.

Saturday, January 15th

Gun practice and alarm after dark which means man-handling guns from unit camp to gun redoubts along thorn boma of camp.

Sunday, January 16th

The General went out with staff to look at new site for camp at Campi-ya-bibi five miles from Maktau towards Mbuyuni.

The Railway line and water pipe have been constructed as far as that, the line being laid at the rate of about 1 and a third miles a day.

We are evidently going to move in force in the next four days to establish a camp on Bibi ridge from which we can attack Mbuyuni.

Monday, January 17th

Crews to pack up kit and tents and sleep out to be ready to move 5 am next morning.

Tuesday, January 18th

Reveille 4.30. At 5.30 we move to Campi-ya-bibi now to be known as Bibi. Loyal North Lancs., Rhodesians and Calcutta Battery all come and camp here.

German Raid on Uganda Railway Attempt to destroy a Bridge

According to mail news from British East Africa, Reuter's Agency states, the Government at Nairobi issued the following official note:

"On April 20, at 2 p. m., a party of Germans, reported as consisting of 15 whites and one *askari*, made an attempt to destroy the girder bridge at mile 218 on Uganda Railway between Makindu and Simba stations. The bridge was guarded by a picquet of the 98th Infantry, but the enemy were able, owing to the thickness of the bush, to creep up unseen and rush the sentry before he could give the alarm to the remainder of his picquet, who were at the time engaged in digging entrenchments in the rear and the men, being taken unawares, were all captured before they could reach their rifles.

"The Germans then blew up portions of the bridge and took the men of the picquet, with their rifles, accoutrements, and telephone, to a distance of about three miles from the scene, where they released them, without their arms. The picquet returned and gave the alarm. The damage done to the bridge is not very extensive, and will not interfere, materially with the traffic. Four 40ft. girders and the centre girder have been damaged, but transshipment was made possible on the day, following the incident, and a temporary diversion of the line has already been effected.

"The Germans, before retiring, tapped the telegraph line between Makindu and Simba, presumably with the telephone apparatus captured from the picquet. It appears that the party were mounted on mules, and were thus able to travel a considerable distance. Now that the rains have set in and water is plentiful, raids of this nature may be expected. All possible precautions are, however, being taken to prevent a second raid being carried out successfully."

MAJOR ARTHUR JOHN BYNG WAVELL M.C. F.R.G.S
1882 - 1916

The name Wavell is mainly associated with the Field Marshall Lord Archibald Wavell, Army Commander and one-time Viceroy of India. His cousin, Arthur Wavell, once described as the "British East African equivalent of T.E. Lawrence," is one of the many extraordinary characters named in Donald's diary.

Arthur Wavell, following in his military family tradition, went to Sandhurst and then obtained a commission in the Welsh Regiment in 1900. Having served with distinction in the South African war, he was appointed by the War Office to report on the unmapped African possessions in the British Empire. He travelled to Swaziland, Tongaland and Northern Zululand, and crossed the Kalahari Desert into Bechuanaland.

In 1906, he resigned his commission to take up hunting in East Africa. He purchased land in Nyali near Mombasa, and became a partner in the Nyali Sisal Company. The rich Arab-Swahili culture clearly fascinated him and he became fluent in Arabic and Swahili, as well as immersing himself in Islamic studies. In 1908, together with two Muslim companions, he embarked on a risky adventure to the Middle East. Disguised as a Zanzibari and travelling on a blackmarket Turkish passport, he was the epoch's last 'Western Pretender' to visit the Islamic holy sites. His book "A Modern Pilgrimmage in Mecca" (which included a preface written by the President of the Royal Geographical Society) was considered a work on par with Gertrude Bell.

After further travels in the Middle East, he returned to Mombasa. When war was declared, in order to defend Mombasa Town, Wavell raised and funded a company called the Arab Rifles, better known as 'Wavell's Arabs.' He recruited his men from the prisons down the coastline and local water carriers. An inspiring and capable leader, Wavell and his corps of 150 men fought in a series of skirmishes along the South Coast. He was badly wounded in the arm in September 1914 but kept on fighting.

On January 8th, 1916, Wavell and fifteen of his men were surprised in an ambush near Mwele Mdogo inland from the Shimba Hills. Despite being severely wounded he kept on firing. He died the next day and is buried, with Lieutenant John Lachland Mackintosh in a small war grave in Mwele Mdogo. Nearby is a memorial to the two NCOs and eleven men who were also killed.

Tucked away beside Fort Jesus' monolithic walls, in a pretty memorial garden, stands an obelisk erected in gratitude by the citizens of Mombasa to Arthur Wavell and his Arab Rifles.

Wednesday, January 19th

Stay in camp. Mounted Infantry about 100 strong, also Belfield's Scouts arrive.

Thursday, January 20th

Aeroplane passed over going to Taveta. Volunteer Maxim Company (from Calcutta) come to Bibi from Maktau.

Major Keene, we hear afterwards was in the aeroplane this morning – the engine failed when over Lake Gippe [Jipe] and had to glider about 1000 feet down when fortunately it started again and returned safely. Two accidents in camp: an M.I. let his pistol off by accident and shot one of the Belfield's Scouts dead, the other case was a cigarette end igniting a bandoleer from which a cartridge exploded and wounded two M.I.

Friday, January 21st

Some of the 5th South African Regiment arrive in camp. We are to attack Mbuyuni tomorrow. We shall be about 4000 strong.

Parker of the I.D. and Major Keene went out last night to see if they could get close to Mbuyuni. They ran into a picket and had rather a hot time of it, Parker having had his mule shot.

Saturday, January 22nd

Reveille 4 am. Armoured cars, Belfield's Scouts and mounted infantry move out in front, Rhodesians in extended order right through the bush, then the batteries which take up positions on the ridge this side of Mbuyuni ready to open fire at about 2500 yard range. 1000 Baluchis, with Parker as guide, were sent out at night to get round behind the camp and catch the Germans retreating – this they failed to do owing to Parker losing his way!! We occupy Mbuyuni without resistance and then follow up the few Germans who were in it – probably 100. The aeroplane flies over and signals a small force there only. We follow up and the flanks had a little scrapping on the next ridge in the thick bush. At one spot we were on the road when there was volleying about 400 yards to our right and all the Mountain Battery mules came stampeding towards us. We could not tell what was happening for a few minutes but it appears a few Germans stuck behind as ambush. The armoured cars chased them out of it and killed quite a few *askaris*. We then returned to Mbuyuni and entrenched there in the old German camp. In the evening some Germans were seen entrenching on the next ridge so we were ordered out. We opened fire at about 1500 yards and burst 4 shrapnel shells over their heads but we heard later from a prisoner that no one was killed. We find in Mbuyuni camp the graves of evidently five white Germans, probably killed the first time we attacked Mbuyuni when we had 150 casualties. Every grave has been covered deep with English cartridge cases. All their trenches were very cleverly dug, some with dummy maxims in!

Sunday, January 23rd

All quiet in the morning. The M.I. go out reconnoitering with the armoured cars. They meet a big patrol of Germans and we are called out. We dash down the road into the bush and shell the bushes on the next ridge where we can see a few Germans. The armoured cars has rescued Parker who was badly wounded and they chivvied a lot of *askaris* and killed those who refused to surrender. One white prisoner is taken and a few natives, one of which was a Madagascan boy who could speak French and Swahili. I had a long talk with him. He told we were to be attacked tomorrow morning which, however, did not come off. We are to attack Serengeti tomorrow, however.

Monday, January 24th

Reveille 4.45. Stand to 5.45. Advance guard: Belfield's Scouts, 1st Rhodesians, No. 1 Light Battery, then the 2 Rhodesians and Mountain Battery and 2 Howitzers. We advance in open order to the ridge this side of Serengeti where we line up ready to bombard.

We find a wounded German *askari* on the way out left from yesterday. He said "his friends" has taken his rifle and has said they would come back tomorrow! We bombarded the camp for an hour and then the Belfield's Scouts and armoured cars entered it to find all the Germans have cleared out. The Baluchis go out later in the day and occupy the camp.

Tuesday, January 25th

We were not called out at all today. An armoured car takes Col. Forrester-Walker out to a point a mile and a half beyond Serengeti Camp to take ranges for shelling Solyta Hill. But, just as they were taking the first range, a maxim opened fire on them at about 300 yards. They managed to rush for the car and all get inside safely right away. The armoured car opened fire with its maxim and killed 2 *askaris*.

THE GENERALS

Von Lettow-Vorbeck was a lucky general, a fact to which he openly admits in his memoirs. One piece of fortune was the initial choice of British commanders. It is debatable whether it was bad luck or judgement that the IEF B force was under the command of a career officer, who had risen up the ranks through seniority rather than merit. General Aitken, an old school Indian army officer, was the not the man to break away from the standard military rule book. His failure to capture Tanga resulted in his summary dismissal and immediate reduction in rank to that of Colonel on half pay for the remainder of the war. Later, it was felt he had been made a scapegoat for the defeat, and was formally exonerated, probably at the instigation of his brother, the newspaper tycoon, Lord Beaverbrook. He was replaced by General 'Wappy' Wapshare, who was cut from the same military cloth as Aitken, but was a solid though uninspiring commander.

During his five months at the helm, he did manage, with his subordinate Tighe, to rid the coastline of the Germans letting Mombasa celebrate a peaceful end to 1914. Wapshare also initiated the operational infrastructure in the Voi-Kilimanjaro area. Under his command work started on a military extension on the railway leading from Voi to Taveta. A water pipeline from the Bura Hills was also constructed. However, British misfortune was compounded by a series of failed attacks including the loss of the recently occupied Jasin and a repulse at Salaita hill. In April 1915, Kitchener gave Wapshare a promotion and transferred him to Mesopotamia.

The Irishman Mickey Tighe was promoted to Commander-in-Chief. A veteran campaigner, Tighe loved a fight (and a drink) and was popular with the troops. To the dismay of his staff officers, he had an aversion to administration. He was also hindered by a lack of troops. In August 1915, out of 15,000 men (including the K.A.R.), only 7,600 were fit enough to fight.

Stewart, the Commander of the IEF C Force, also had campaign experience. He was a safe and capable commander who was meticulous in carrying out orders. Perhaps Donald's unflattering remarks about Stewart were rooted in part to the existing antipathy between the Indian officers and the settlers. The "Poona Poona" brigade, were condescending to the settlers and labelled the administration as 'parochial' in both social and military matters. Military hierarchy meant that the more experienced K.A.R. and E.A.M.R. were subordinate to the Indian officers.

1915 ended with the encouraging news of the arrival of fresh troops from South Africa and a proper General Officer in Command, Smith-Dorrien. The War Office was taking the campaign seriously. Smith-Dorrien had a respected track record with African experience having fought in the Zulu and Boer Wars. En route to Cape Town, Smith-Dorrien began the campaign plans in earnest. However, he became seriously ill with pneumonia and had to stand down. In his place, the South African Jan Smuts took control. A natural leader, Smuts was known for his energy, personal courage and impatience. He had proved himself as a commando fighter in the Boer Army against the British but was now a career politician. There were doubts about his suitability and even Cranworth remarked that a professional soldier would have been a better choice.

In anticipation of Smuts' imminent arrival, Tighe (apparently acting on orders from Smith-Dorrien) made the decision to attack Salaita 'the cork in the bottle' triggering the push into German East Africa. From Donald's first hand account, it was a fiasco. General Wilfrid Malleson was responsible for planning the advance. A staff officer rather than battle commander, he had been put in command of the Voi area in May 1915 and had already notched up one disaster at Mbuyuni in July that year, resulting in the casualties of 170 men. He was attacked by a German patrol and had it not been

for the heroic actions of Subadar Ghulan Haidar of the 130th Baluchis, Malleson would have lost his life.

Described as having a fondness for champagne and women, Malleson seemed to be universally disliked. Meinertzhagen described him as "… a bad man, clever as a monkey, but hopelessly unreliable and with a nasty record behind him. He is by far the cleverest man out here, but having spent all his service in an Ordinance Office, knows very little about active operations and still less of the usual courtesies amongst British officers. He comes from a class which would wreck the Empire to advance himself. … [He] is loathed and despised as an overbearing bully, ill mannered, and a rotten soldier."

Smuts arrived on the 12th February 1916 to a scene of devastation. Apart from appointing Jacobus Van Deventer as his second-in-command, he had not tampered with Smith-Dorrien's chain of command. Of Malleson, he said:

> "I regret to say that after the Salaita fiasco on the 12 February there is very little confidence in the fighting ability of Malleson and a change in the command of the 1st East African Brigade is also desirable; Tighe considers him a capable administrator and I hope his talents could be better employed by the War Office in an administrative capacity."

The battle at Latema Nek saw Malleson being driven away from the field, apparently suffering from stomach pains. He was quickly moved, with a promotion, to prevent the "Bolshevists" from gaining a stronghold in the Middle East.

Smuts retained Tighe in his reshuffle of the army. When Tighe was recalled by the War Office, Smuts was genuinely disappointed. The position was given to General Hoskins. Stewart's steady leadership was not appreciated. Smuts heaped vitriol on him and he was ignominiously transferred. He later became the Governor of Aden.

"Slim" (or sly) Jannie as he was called in South Africa, may not have been an ideal choice. In his defence, he had been given the unenviable task of commanding a polyglot army of over 50,000 soldiers, in an unmapped and hostile environment. The little red book of military tactics, so beloved by the British officers, was redundant in this war. Ignoring advice, Smuts believed the rainy season could be no worse than the conditions in France. When the rains came the men and mechanised transport were immobilised, bogged down in the sticky glutinous mud. Smuts has been criticized for the administration of chain of supplies that rendered men to half rations and for leading from the front (sometimes too far in front leaving the British military machine struggling to keep up). However, he did succeed in reclaiming British territory and moving the campaign into German East Africa. He was in charge of the East African operations until March 1917, when the Prime Minister of the Union of South Africa, Louis Botha, appointed him to represent the South African Union at the Imperial War Conference in London.

Above: Brigadier General Stewart on left with Sir Henry Belfield.

Wednesday, January 26th

Rather a wet morning. Mbuyuni Station being laid out – rail and pipe line reach camp. We were to have bombarded Solyta but owing to ranges etc. not having been taken we could not go out.

(Boy arrives).

Thursday, January 27th

2 aeroplanes go to bomb Solyta and Taveta. One fails to return and we hear the other came down owing to engine trouble about a mile and a half beyond Serengeti camp on Langoro [Njoro] drift. He may have been brought down by rifle fire for he was heavily fired on as he landed in the bush. He had to run for his life chased by a small patrol and managed to get away back to Serengeti camp He burnt his machine before he left. 2000 more South Africans arrive in the camp with General Beves. Smith-Dorrien's staff officers arrive in Nairobi.

Friday, January 28th

Intensely hot and a gallon of water per man and that very tarry owing to new pipe line. Some of the new South African troops arriving from Maktau actually come round asking if they can buy water from us. We manage to give a bottle to some of them as we get an extra allowance for the cars.

The 5th South African Regiment comes in with bagpipes and bugle, and drum band.

Various shots fired intermittently all night by South African pickets at moving bushes and jackals probably.

Saturday, January 29th

Calcutta Battery and Howitzers (4 inch) have to return to Maktau owing to their members refusing to drink tarry water. We hear that Smith-Dorrien is ill in South Africa.

Motor lorries, Reos and Packhards, carry water to the troops at Serengeti. Thunder all round and a few showers of rain; otherwise extremely hot.

ARMOURED CARS

The steel plated armoured cars contained a three-man-crew. The driver sat on the floor while two gunners operated the gun (a water-cooled Vickers.303) mounted on the turret. It must have been very uncomfortable and incredibly hot inside.

Capell, in his history of the 2nd Rhodesia Regiment in East Africa, described them as:

> 'Those armoured cars are irresistible, huge Rolls-Royce machines, heavily armoured, four tons of silent-night and noiseless engines bounding over the velt, over bush and stump, through brushwood and grass, into the midst of a body of infantry, where they begin to spit fire and bark bullets, themselves invulnerable – as a khaki-clad juggernaut they ride over those that resist, shoot down those that run. There is no reason why two such cars in open country should not entirely destroy a whole battalion, provided their ammunition last out. We are very glad the Germans have none; a car with a pom-pom or light Hotchkiss would seem to be their antidote and bugbear.

Von Lettow did not believe of their existence, but his German *askaris* watching them through binoculars, nicknamed the cars "Kifaru" or rhinos and believed they contained evil spirits.

Sunday, January 30th

It rained heavily last night, but we are kept dry sleeping in our motors. The 5th, 6th & 7th South African regiments are now here. All have bands. The 5th plays at church service held in the open.

Monday January 31st

More rain. Lecture on gunnery. Small force of farmers attack Serengeti but are driven off with few casualties – gun casualties 2 Baluchis killed.

Above: Donald with the Loyal North Lancs in No. 1 Light Battery, 1915.
The armoured cars might have been a novelty. On the other hand, a captured German prisoner, being taken past one of the British artillery parks, remarked: "The movable armament from the Ark, I should imagine."

On the March from Maktau
with the Loyal North Lancs

FEBRUARY 1916

Tuesday February 1st

Two of our Intelligence Department rode out with hope of seeing the Kasigau force which is supposed to have evacuated Kasigau and to be returning to Taveta.

They come back and report having seen the column a mile and a half long. One of them personally tells me he saw some of the men on horses, some oxen etc. etc. Eventually, however, it is proved they only saw a column of dust – probably zebra! The M.I. go out the next day and find no tracks of troops.

Wednesday, February 2nd

Wet day but hear rumours of "something doing tomorrow!"

Thursday, February 3rd

Reveille 4 am. Battery ready 5 am. 1600 South Africans left camp 7pm last night to make big detour through the bush, cross the Langoro [Njoro] river low down and get behind a German outpost supposed to be camped on Langoro [Njoro] drift. We are to move along the road through Serengeti camp and attack from the side and then reconnoitre round Solyta hill. The Lancs, 5th and 6th South Africans, Belfield's Scouts, M.I., Calcutta and Mountain Batteries and ourselves move out in extended order and sweep right through only to find the 1600 South Africans on their way back not having caught the Huns. Mountain Battery cross the drift and shell Solyta hill. We saw the Germans go out of block house and retreat. The pioneers had to cut out the drift before we could cross so we did not get into action. Column retired, our battery covering retreat.

Friday, February 4th

All quiet

Saturday, February 5th

Railway survey party covered by 1000 South Africans go out to drift. Mine exploded in the road this side. Fortunately no one hurt. Evidently fuse was too long and exposed as some of the South Africans had walked over it when those behind heard it sizzle and scattered when up it went.

Flags flying gaily on Solyta block house.

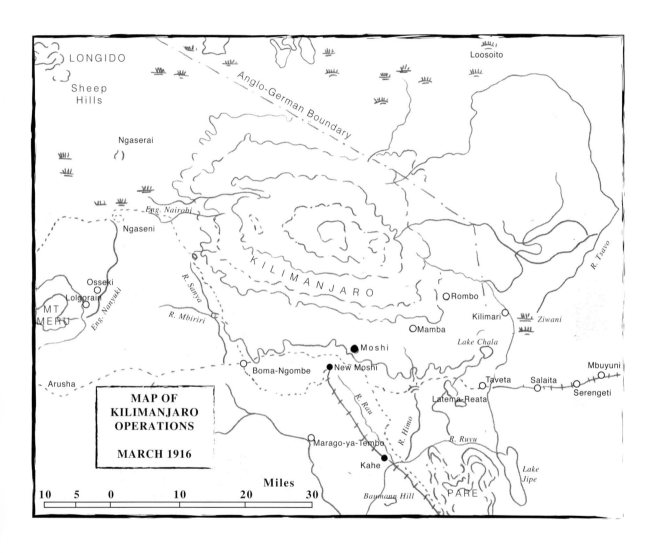

LONGIDO

Sheep
Hills

Loosoito

Anglo-German Boundary

Ngaserai

Eng. Nairobi

Ngaseni

K I L I M A N J A R O

R. Sanya

R. Tsavo

Osseki

○ Rombo

Lolgorain

Eng. Nanyuki

MT
MERU

R. Mbiriri

Kilimari

Ziwani

○ Mamba

Lake Chala

○ Moshi

Boma-Ngombe

● New Moshi

Arusha

Mbuyuni

Taveta

Salaita

Latema-Reata

Serengeti

**MAP OF
KILIMANJARO
OPERATIONS**

MARCH 1916

R. Rau

R. Himo

R. Ruvu

Marago-ya-Tembo

Kahe

*Lake
Jipe*

Miles

| 10 | 5 | 0 | 10 | 20 | 30 |

Baumann Hill

PARE

Sunday, February 6th

Royal Flying Corps arrive. They have 12 B.E. aeroplanes on the way – numerous Crossley motor lorries and brakes and, I believe, about 100 men.

Monday, February 7th

A Rhodesian force covering the Railway survey at Langoro drift meet a German patrol. Rhodesians get their maxim going and account for several. But bush is so thick it is impossible to tell how many were killed. They seem to have crossed the drift a few hundred yards in front of the force and to have blundered right on to the Germans.

Langoro drift had been mined by the Germans but they were all seen to by the engineers.

Tuesday, February 8th

We hear that a strange, loose mule was seen running round Serengeti camp and it is thought this is Hall's mule but there is no news of Hall yet.

Wednesday, February 9th

The five new Reo cars take out our battery for the first time. They go out with other troops to cover the six 1st pioneers (Indian) who are to make 3 crossings over Langoro. Lavender and I volunteer to go with them on the chance of a scrap but only a few of the flankers have a small brush with a small out-picket from Solyta.

One of the new B.E. aeroplanes goes up in the evening and flies beautifully.

Thursday, February 10th

The 8th South African Regiment arrives – also Howitzers – back from Maktau. At 4 pm in the afternoon a German column is reported a mile and half from camp moving toward Lake Gippe. Armoured cars, M.I., and Belfield Scouts all dash out only to find a big herd of game!

Scouting in East Africa
Officer's Adventures

From no part of the war area is news so scarce as from East Africa. The following extracts from the letter of an officer servicing there are accordingly valuable, especially as he tells shortly, of scouting exploits that had more of a spice of danger in them. The final passages were written early in February.

I came back two days to the main camp from my patrol, having gone into German territory to scout. As I did not want to be seen or heard if I could help it, I only went on foot, with six men, and managed to see a good deal of the country, without being seen myself, on the first day. But on the second I went to reconnoitre an outpost consisting of three grass huts inside a thorn fence, which is only occasionally used as a post of observation by the enemy, and carefully scouted to see whether there was anyone there by dodging behind trees and crawling through the shoulder-high grass. There is a tree at the centre of the enclosure on the top of which is a little grass hut from which the native German levies keep a look-out. As I got within 300 yards of this place I suddenly saw two khaki-clad figures, one on the ladder leading up to the hut, and one just going in. Realising that they would see me directly they reached the top of the ladder, I took a shot at and dropped the one who was half way up. The other scuttled down before I could get a shot at him, and evidently gave the alarm, for, as I came out of the long grass into the path leading from the enclosure, I was fired upon by a German native soldier, who missed me. He fired a second time, but made another rotten shot, and I don't know where his bullet went. Aiming at the smoke made by his rifle, I fired and dropped a man. We then retreated as I expected the Germans would be out in force on hearing the firing, but I suppose they did not go far, as we never saw nor heard them. So I went back to camp and reported accordingly.

The same day orders came in for us to refit at Nairobi. If, and when, we get in, I don't suppose we shall be at Nairobi much more than a week before returning here, after which I suppose there will be a nearer possibility of an advance into German East Africa.

Fort Perched on a Hill

I left off my letter as some Masai came in with the news that some Germans had come down to a place about 15 miles away, so I collected about forty of our men and went out, headed by the Masai runners, but as it took me four hours to reach the place, on arrival I found the enemy had cleared out two hours previously owing to their being fired upon by the Masai, who wounded two white men, one dangerously. So I was too late for that shauri! But we picked up a German map, which had been dropped by them, and which will be extremely useful to our people. I think it possible that the Germans will come down to get their own back off the Masai so have moved to a better camp, where I shall stay at any rate till he returns from Nairobi, where he has gone to refit.

We are perched on a little hill here. Nearly all the country round is burnt brown by the hot sun and rainless days, which we get at this time of year. A stone wall has been built round the top of the hill leaving an irregular space, in which we have built one long grass hut as our mess-room. In the corner of the hut I have had a charpoi built out of rough sticks, on the top of which is a thick layer of grass. Here I spread my long brown canvas valise, stuffing one end in order to make a pillow. Here I sleep fairly peacefully, occasionally getting up to have a look round at the sentries and a survey over the moonlit landscape.

By the by, will you send me a Bible and a Prayer Book, the former with references in the margin and the latter with hymns. I have lost mine, and we occasionally have terrific discussions as to how some psalm or hymn goes.

Friday, February 11th

SERENGETI

The Reo lorries and South Africans take over Battery and we are attached to Divisional Headquarters Staff.

Nearly all troops move to Serengeti. Bands playing etc. They must be 200 Reo lorries at work beside trains etc. I have a good look round Serengeti camp in the evening and examine all the German trenches. The outside trench is 3 miles round and must require 1000 men at least to man it. Everything is very well designed with a few bomb-proofs etc., but as the Germans only had a few tanks of water which had to be carted out from Taveta, the whole camp must be a gigantic bluff!

Saturday, February 12th

ATTACK ON SOLYTA [SALAITA]

All troops move out early. General Beves with the South Africans in advance guard, then Volunteer Maxim gun section, Lancs., Baluchis, Rhodesians, all Batteries. The idea is to take Solyta and occupy it, so much so that kit was taken out. I had to take some Headquarters boxes out etc. etc. I did not leave till 8 am and got to a point half-mile this side of drift by 8.10 just as they commenced shelling the hill. The hill sticks up out of the plain – a beautiful target – with the block house on the top with 2 flags flying, a big trench round it, and three other tiers round the hill and thick bush at the bottom. We plaster the sides of the top with shells for 2 hours at a range of about 5000 yards. I was on the road about 500 yards from the big guns for the first three hours and then crossed the drift about 1000 yards above the road and go down about a mile when I find that the general order for retiring had been given and I only just get back in time as the Germans had sent round a flanking party and also started shelling the retreat. I saw some of the shell holes made by the German guns and some of the shells had hardly burst. They were evidently naval 7-pounders, probably only 3 guns but we never located them. Their shells, I believe, only killed one of our men by a direct hit. The South Africans (7th) let us down by retiring from the first – at they first volleying. The Germans had got down into the thick bush at the foot of Solyta, called up 2,000 reinforcements from Taveta and had heaps of Maxims, pompoms etc. in trenches which certainly surprised our South Africans. Our fault was shelling the top of the hill which was naturally empty and leaving the bushes alone. Communication failed between units. 2 armoured cars did good work. Our casualties were about 160 mostly South Africans. They chased us right back to rail-head where we had water tanks ready full of water. These had to be broken in and abandoned and were further spied by the Germans at night. All troops suffering a lot from thirst and the failure of the right wing. When I went a mile beyond the drift I saw horses and mules running about loose in the thick bush and loads of ammunition etc. lying about. One Maxim of the W.M.C.C. was under the bush and they told me they were the remains of the right flank. Rhodesians and Baluchis and No. 1 Light Battery fought an excellent rearguard action. No. 1 Light Battery had lots of shells round them and one car hit. On the whole a bad defeat for us as we had approximately 6000 men, 18 guns and 36 Maxims and the Germans had three 7-pounders, 3000 men, maxims etc. unknown.

Sunday, February 13th

South African brigade returns to Mbuyuni

Monday, February 14th

MBUYUNI

In camp at Headquarters at Mbuyuni. We hear that Reggie Hall is a wounded prisoner in the hands of Germans.

General Tighe and staff arrive. Thank God.

Tuesday, February 15th

A third 4-inch gun comes. The South African brigade, which is all in the camp, is undergoing a course of general physical training as few of them are really fit. Aeroplanes go up in the evening with bombs for Solyta but I have not yet heard what result. The 4th South African Horse, 700 strong, arrive in camp that evening – full of confidence etc. They do nothing but quote what they did in German South West Africa (G.S.W.A.). When told that there was more fighting last Saturday than in the whole of the G.S.W.A. Campaign, they begin to take things a little more seriously.

The Volunteer Calcutta Battery.

THE EMPIRE'S ARMY

"Since Alexander of Macedonia descended on to the plains of Africa, there can never have been such a strange and heterogeneous an army such as this."

Roberty Dolbey, Sketches from an East African Campaign

It has been disputed as to whether von Lettow-Vorbeck's strategy of diverting troops made any difference to the allied numbers on the Western Front. However, he did manage to draw in troops of widely diverse nationalities. Apart from the Belgian and Portuguese Allies, the British Army comprised of Indians, Rhodesians, South Africans, Nigerians, West Indians as well as soldiers from the Gold Coast and Sierra Leone.

The West African soldiers entered the theatre in 1917, when the bulk of the European and Indian troops were exhausted and too ill to be an effective fighting force.

The first British Battalion to fight in the East African Campaign, the 2nd Loyal North Lancs, were part of the doomed IEF 'B' who sailed over from India to repel the Germans out of East Africa. After the fiasco at Tanga, the battalion was absorbed into a number of units including Cole's Scouts (which were later incorporated into the Mounted Infantry Company) and Donald's company in 1916, Logan's Battery.

By the beginning of 1916, the soldiers in 2nd Loyal North Lancs had fought in battles on Lake Victoria, the South Coast and at Mbuyuni. Worn down by constant attacks of malaria and dysentery as well as beriberi and malnutrition, they were sent to South Africa for recuperation. They returned to Mombasa in August 1916 and together with reinforcements from England, travelled to Kilwa. A few months later, still ravaged by illness, they were transferred to Eygpt. A core of 120 fit men stayed behind under the newly formed 2nd Loyal North Lancs Machine Gun Company. They marched to Kibata, joining Donald, to fight in one of the longest and fiercest engagements of the campaign.

During 1917, the Loyal North Lancs continued to fight in the South of German East Africa. However, at the end of the year, they were posted back to England after the decision was taken to replace European and Indian soldiers with hardier *askari* and African forces. (The recommendation to recruit local men was mooted by Cranworth at the outset and had been firmly rejected by Lord Kitchener). A plaque in Nairobi Cathedral commemorates the men of the 2nd Loyal North Lancashire Regiment who lost their lives on African soil.

Governor Belfield's telegram to the Colonial Office on the 4th August 1914 requesting defence for his Protectorate was a hot potato tossed from the Colonial Office to India and from India to the Committee of Imperial Defence who formed a sub-committee, named the Offensive Sub-Committee. This sub-committee recommended that two Indian Expeditionary Forces (IEF) be raised. Using troops from 29th and 30th Baluchis and the Imperial Service Army It was decided that IEF 'B' would attack Tanga in the South and IEF 'C' go to the Kilimanjaro region in the North.

More Indian troops were sent to East Africa including the 129th Baluchis, (who had been fighting in Flanders), the 130th Baluchis, and 40th Pathans (the Forty Thieves). They were joined by the Kashmir Rifles, a squadron of the 17th Indian Cavalry and a volunteer Calcutta Battery. Fresh from fighting in Flanders, the 129th Baluchis were demoralized and depleted in numbers. They soon gained respect on the battlefield for using the least amount of ammunition, whilst accounting for the greatest number of casualties.

Once Smuts was put in charge, he drafted troops from South Africa. Whilst this army included seasoned officers and soldiers from the Boer Wars, the South African volunteers were raw teenage recruits. Their introduction to fighting during this battle for Salaita was equivalent to the bloody initiation of the British army at Tanga. The Baluchis returned the weaponry lost by the South Africans apparently, with a note that read: "with the compliments of the 130th Baluchis. May we request that you do not any longer refer to our sepoys as coolies."

The 2nd Rhodesian Regiment were sent a much more flattering missive, commending them for their assistance and expressing the wish "that they would fight together once more". Raised from 800 volunteers, the 2nd Rhodesians were commanded by Lieutenant Colonel Algernan Essex Capell D.S.O. (who later wrote the history of the unit) and proved themselves to be a formidable fighting force. Not happy with the scouts that had been provided for them, they also brought in their own native scouts. Like all the other regiments, disease and hunger took its toll and the Rhodesians were recalled to Salisbury in 1917 where they were later disbanded.

Wednesday, February 16th

Trelterney (spelling) comes through from Serengeti camp and reports that at 9 pm and 1 am evidently about 50 Germans poured volleys into the camp – bright moonlight – general pandemonium but no one hit that we can hear of. Germans also blew up the line again. He says that a German officer through on a mule with a white flag but was stopped outside the camp. He came to ask for medical stores. He said their casualties were 500!! It appears the Rhodesian reconnoitering on Sunday found 8 South Africans in the bush with their throats cut. Still 28 missing! Our casualties now must be about 200, including 21 killed. A woodcutting party just out of Serengeti camp finds bodies of 35 German *askaris*, evidently killed by our shell fire on January 24th.

Thursday, February 17th

The rest of the 3rd battalion, K.A.R. passed through to Serengeti. General Tighe leaves here to go to Mombasa to meet General Smuts. The aeroplane practice dropping bombs close to camp as many of those dropped on Taveta have not exploded. One 90-lb bomb of TNT makes a hole about 8' x 3' x 3' deep. Very hot indeed in camp and flies getting bad.

All quiet here. Also at Serengeti. Captain Powell tells us it is arranged for us to go back to the battery. I have, however, some days ago written to Martin to see he can interview Wedgewood and get me a commission in the Armoured Cars.

Friday, February 18th

The Sergeant of the Light Battery was in here today and tells us that last Saturday one shell pitched within 3 yards of the guns but did not explode, another hit the tree some of the drivers were under and stuck there, and many passed over their heads when they were covering the retreat. It appears the 7th South Africans threw away 160 rifles and lost many thousand rounds of ammunition, their chief excuse was they were carrying wounded! I saw many wounded thrown on lorries and bumped back to Serengeti as there were only 3 Ford ambulance cars*. Butt flew over Solyta today but could not see a soul, probably all hiding in trenches!

Saturday, February 19th

Activity of enemy on Solyta reported by aeroplanes.

Henry Ford had stipulated that his cars were forbidden for use in active military service but could be utilised for transport and ambulances.

AEROPLANES IN THE EAST AFRICA CAMPAIGN

Unlike some army officers, who believed that aeroplanes were no substitute for horses, Smuts was a strong supporter of the Flying Corps. He had started an air wing in South Africa in 1913 and planes had been used with some success in the South West Africa campaign. Prior to Smuts' appointment, the Royal Naval Air Squadron used seaplanes to hunt down the Konigsberg in the Rufiji Delta and in October 1915, under Tighe's command, an air field was established at Mbuyuni. By the end of year there were eight planes stationed at the base. They were used for bombing missions and reconnaissance (wildlife photographer, Cherry Kearton, was transferred to take aerial photographs). In 1916 numbers swelled when the South African Royal Air Squadron joined the campaign. A new airbase was built at Maktau and was then moved to Morogoro and later onto Dar-es-Salaam. By 1917 the air force was staffed by over 350 men, who served as airmen, mechanics, carpenters and armourers for a fleet of aircraft including Voisins, BE2cs, BE2ds.

Flying in East Africa has its challenges even for modern bush pilots so how the pilots flew those rudimentary planes is unimaginable. High altitude and the turbulence from the ranges of hills meant the planes could often only take off at dawn. Landing strips had to be cleared in the thick bush, which became unusable in the rains and dust got into everything. The pilots, just as prone to malaria and dysentery as the army on the ground, also suffered severe sunburn.

As the war progressed, the local Africans became accustomed to the 'birds that dropped iron eggs' and ran away to safety when they spotted the planes. There were no aerial dog fights as the only German owned bi-plane crashed in the early months of the war. During December in 1916, the Germans were astounded to watch the Allied planes bomb their own army in Kibata. It transpired that they were dropping cigarettes for Christmas.

The press clipping reporting the contribution to the aeroplane fund, was only part of a large fundraising campaign. British territories in Africa donated 274 planes, which at a cost of £2,000 (the equivalent of £548,000 today) per plane was quite remarkable. Some of the donations came from African chiefs who gave cattle in lieu of cash.

After the war, aeroplanes gained popularity in East Africa as an attractive way to cover the vast distances. Some of Kenya's famous personalities took up flying, most notably the celebrated aviatrix Beryl Markham.

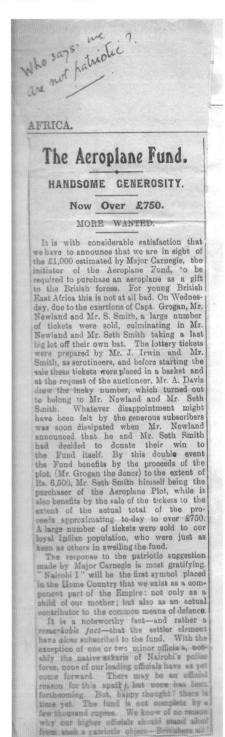

Who says we are not patriotic?

AFRICA.

The Aeroplane Fund.

HANDSOME GENEROSITY.

Now Over £750.

MORE WANTED.

It is with considerable satisfaction that we have to announce that we are in sight of the £1,000 estimated by Major Carnegie, the initiator of the Aeroplane Fund, to be required to purchase an aeroplane as a gift to the British forces. For young British East Africa this is not at all bad. On Wednesday, due to the exertions of Capt. Grogan, Mr. Newland and Mr. S. Smith, a large number of tickets were sold, culminating in Mr. Newland and Mr. Seth Smith taking a last big lot off their own bat. The lottery tickets were prepared by Mr. J. Irwin and Mr. Smith, as scrutineers, and before starting the sale these tickets were placed in a basket and at the request of the auctioneer, Mr. A. Davis drew the lucky number, which turned out to belong to Mr. Newland and Mr. Seth Smith. Whatever disappointment might have been felt by the generous subscribers was soon dissipated when Mr. Newland announced that he and Mr. Seth Smith had decided to donate their win to the Fund itself. By this double event the Fund benefits by the proceeds of the plot, (Mr. Grogan the donor) to the extent of Rs. 6,500, Mr. Seth Smith himself being the purchaser of the Aeroplane Plot, while it also benefits by the sale of the tickets to the extent of the actual total of the proceeds approximating to-day to over £750. A large number of tickets were sold to our loyal Indian population, who were just as keen as others in swelling the fund.

The response to the patriotic suggestion made by Major Carnegie is most gratifying. "Nairobi I" will be the first symbol placed in the Home Country that we exist as a component part of the Empire: not only as a child of our mother; but also as an actual contributor to the common means of defence. It is a noteworthy fact—and rather a remarkable fact—that the settler element have alone subscribed to the fund. With the exception of one or two minor officials, notably the native askaris of Nairobi's police force, none of our leading officials have as yet come forward. There may be an official reason for this apathy, but none has been forthcoming. But, happy thought! there is time yet. The fund is not complete by a few thousand rupees. We know of no reason why our higher officials should stand aloof from such a patriotic object.—Britishers all

67

A small reconnaissance was made from Serengeti towards Solyta. 2 armoured cars halted on the road just this side of Langoro drift and turned around there. There was also a Repo lorry for telegraph cable with them. Just as they were moving off there was a tremendous explosion – a mine being exploded by the rear wheel of the lorry hitting it. The hind part of the lorry was lifted a bit off the ground but no damage done! The armoured cars and men had been walking and moving and over it for some minutes without setting it off. I heard the explosion and saw the immense cloud of earth and dust thrown up from here (Mbuyuni) 7 miles away!

Sunday, February 20th

Arrival of General Smuts at Mbuyuni with General Tighe – flourish of trumpets, guard of honour, bands etc. He motors straight through side of Langoro drift from where he has a good look at Solyta. He leaves Mbuyuni by train again at about 3.30.

Monday, February 21st

I have a long talk with Pretorius of the I.D. He left camp on Saturday night with 600 of the 4th South African Horse and rode to Lumi river (leaving Solyta 4 miles on his left), left most of the men there, and took on 2 officers and 3 men to the Taveta road and rode to within 1000 yards of Taveta! Stayed there 3 minutes and galloped back as hard as he could. He was watched by the Germans from 2 small forts, Charlo and ? [Donald's questionmark]. But his was too big a force to surround. The idea was to see if columns and guns could be taken to attack Taveta from behind and so isolate Solyta – quite feasibly. He is only I.D. man who knows the country and can speak the truth!

Tuesday, February 22nd

Heard a big explosion every early this morning about 4 o'clock but have not yet heard the cause. Ascertained afterwards that it was an attempt to blow up the line near rail-head just beyond Serengeti. It appears that only one sleeper was slightly blown out of place.

Wednesday, February 23rd

All quiet.

165 of the 4th South African Horse rode out (with Pretorius as guide) to have a look at the German camp at the south end of Jippe. They came on it at 5 am in the morning.

THE ARMY BANDS

The distant cacophony of the army bands striking up must have alerted the enemy to any new development in an allied army camp. It seems that any advance or important arrival was heralded by the bands playing. When the army marched out of Maktau for the Battle of Mbuyuni, all the military bands heralded the departure - so much for an element of surprise!

The K.A.R. were very proud of their band. In the "History of the King's African Rifles," Moyse-Barlett devotes a whole appendix to the formation of the K.A.R. band. When the Loyal North Lancs arrived in Voi in 1916 they were accompanied by their own bandmaster, who was later attached to the 3rd K.A.R. He taught his recruits how to play music and the musicians were soon in hot demand. Members of the 3rd K.A.R. band played on recruitment tours and at charity concerts for the war effort. In 1918, the K.A.R. received a bequest from the Leeke family whose son had died of blackwater fever in Voi. With this and funds raised from the canteen profits, they invested in brass instruments. In 1919, kitted out in kilts and using their new instruments, they welcomed home the battalions returning for demobilization.

The Germans sent about 12 *askaris* out into to the open hoping no doubt that the South African Horse would ride at them and then the Germans concealed in the bush, would open fire on them with their maxims. The South African House see the ruse and leave them alone. They could not find out the German strength owing to the dense bush.

Thursday, February 24th

All quiet

Dine at the Royal Flying Corps Mess.

We hear that General Smuts is coming here on Sunday so we expect to attack Taveta next week. Very hot and general a rain storm in the afternoons.

Steam-boring plant starts work by the waterhole in Mbuyuni vlei.

Friday, February 25th

3 Indians found a mine on the railway near Bibi. When digging it up, it exploded and killed them all.

4th South African Horse, with Pretorius as guide, were out last night again to find where the bush is thinnest so that they can cut a road through it to the south of Lake Jippe from which point it is only 10 miles to a new station the Germans have built on the Tanga-Moshi line.

The Germans again blew up the line in 2 or 3 places between Serengeti and Langoro drift but did no damage to speak of.

Rained very heavily last night.

Saturday, February 26th

All quiet here – a lot of trains coming with oxen and carts, also some of the 1st South African Horse.

This afternoon, about 3 pm, three German officers and two or 3 boys appeared, dressed in our South African uniforms, at the head tanks of the water supply in the Bura hills about three miles from the camp which were guarded(!) by one old pioneer (too decrepit

MAJOR PHILIP JACOBUS PRETORIUS C.M.G. D.S.O. & BAR
1877 - 1945

"I must have been born with the divine unrest of adventure"

The legendary P.J. Pretorius, hunter, African adventurer and nomad, was credited with having no nerves and a clairvoyant sense for self-preservation. Born into a voertreeker family, his incredible life story starts with his first job riding transport for the British South Africa Company at the age of 16 in Cecil Rhodes' bid for Matabeleland. Unhindered by borders or laws, he then travelled throughout Southern and Eastern Africa hunting elephant, living among pygmies, cannibals among other tribes and honing his bushcraft. He harboured a deep hatred for the Germans in East Africa. With justification as they had put him in prison, revoked his hunting licence and confiscated his farm on the Rufiji. He took his revenge by poaching enough ivory to cover the cost of his stolen farm. Labelled an outlaw, he was shot in both legs by a patrol of German *askari*s, and was only saved by his gun bearers and porters.

Gaunt and sallow-skinned from frequent bouts of malaria, he often passed as an Arab trader. In this guise Pretorius evaded, and even gathered information from, the German *Askari*. On one occasion he even managed to board the Konigsberg. His reconnaissance resulted in the destruction of the Konigsberg in the swampy maze of the Rufiji Delta. He spent most of his war deep behind enemy lines. In his memoir he rather chillingly describes his war career as "still following jungle trails, still the hunter, only the quarries were humans instead of animals."

When he met Donald, he had only recently been appointed as Chief Scout to Smuts. Under his own orders, he then followed the German trail along the Pangani River, and down south beyond Lindi, accompanied by ten porters and captured German *askaris* (now wearing British uniform). Despite the threat of reprisals and carrying a price on his head, Pretorius relied on the local Africans for much of his information.

Delegated as the scout in charge of leading the 25th Fusiliers to Behobeho, Pretorius was replaced by Frederick Courtenay Selous. It was on this mission that Selous was killed by a German sniper.

His clairvoyancy held out and Pretorius died in Pretoria in 1945, as a relatively old man. His adventures were fictionalized in "Shout at the Devil" by Wilbur Smith.

Above, P.J. Pretorius from the frontispiece of his autobiography.

for anything else so, I suppose, they thought he was competent to look after the water supply of a whole division!!). After taking tea with him, they held him up with revolvers and proceeded to blow up the tanks and filtering apparatus and then decamped! Another party blew up another water tank at the same time a few miles off. We hear later on in the evening that one German has been caught. We hope he will be shot for wearing our uniforms! Tanks etc. were all mended in 12 hours and we got water through again here very soon.

A later, more correct, report of the above is that one of the Germans, after having hurt his knee, returned to the Pioneers' hut where he was captured. A second German was captured later on but I have not heard how it occurred.

Sunday, February 27th

Reports of a small scrap beyond the 2-yard drift in which 3 German *askaris* were taken prisoner but no definite details are in yet. 4th S.A.H were out in the bush in various directions trying to intercept the Germans who blew up the Bura water tanks.

Aeroplanes have been photographing Solyta and Taveta for the last 2 or 3 days

Monday, February 28th

Yesterday's scrap near Solyta – we seem to have taken 6 German *askaris* prisoner and killed 2 or 3 more.

All quiet here.

Tuesday, February 29th

General Smuts arrives with his brother as Staff Captain.

A small force of King's African Rifles (K.A.R.) reconnoitering from Serengeti encountered a German patrol. As they had two maxims, I understand our force retired with 9 K.A.R. *askaris* wounded and one European motor cyclist. This is only from third-handed rumours in from Serengeti which are always unreliable.

Aeroplanes dropped 4 bombs on Taveta last evening was [sic] fired on by field guns.

1st and 2nd South African Horse continue to arrive by train.

Above: Salvaging wood from a bombed train.
Below: A newly fitted armoured train.

No Thomas Cook Holiday

MARCH 1916

Wednesday, March 1st

We are all wondering when the advance is going to take place – it must be either the end of this week or beginning of next. The Division is practically complete with 3 brigades of infantry, artillery and about 2500 cavalry, thousands of 2-wheeled ox Scotch carts, mule wagons and motor lorries and cars of all descriptions. Very little sickness in camp but horse and cattle beginning to look poor. So the sooner and quicker the "push" comes the better. Photos of Solyta and Taveta show it very strongly held and all between Soltya and Taveta nothing but one-man rifle pits.

Thursday, March 2nd

All quiet and very hot indeed.

Friday, March 3rd

All quiet

Have to go to Serengeti Camp in the morning,

Had a long talk with Cranworth and Isaacson in the evening about getting a commission. They strongly advise us to stay put where we are as commissions are being given to all sorts of people and one would probably be put in the ammunition column which is not a desirable job.

Saturday, March 4th

Field day of batteries, ammunition columns etc. – inspected by the General.

2 Caudrons which have been at Maktau all this time fly over here to stay.

Sunday, March 5th

4th Brigades comes into Mbuyuni

Monday, March 6th

Great move Mbuyuni to Serengeti

Two British Soldiers go Lion Hunting
Fine Bag in German Colony

The following are extracts from letters received from Geoffrey Catchpole, grandson of Mrs Fisk of 8 Wellington Road, Brighton. The letters to hand have given much pleasure, no news having been received from him for several weeks. Mr. Catchpole is in the South African Mounted Rifles:-

Lion Shooting for Recreation

"The camp we are in is fairly foul and extremely windy at night. Oswyn rolled in the day before yesterday and left yesterday morning, after having 'brekker' with me at the observation post. I did not see much of him during the evening he was here, as I had arranged to sit up with a man called Billiter to try and shoot some lions that had killed our one remaining bullock (for eating).

B. and I went down to our tiny thorn Zariba about a quarter to seven, arranged our blankets and had just started our final cigarette before starting our watch when we heard crunching outside, and I could just dimly see a lioness four yards away. I fired and she fell with a bullet through the brain. I then went to sleep, as the next shot was Billiter's. About midnight he fired three shots at another lioness, one of which hit her through the kidneys. She went about 100 yards and died. We both then slept until three-thirty, when I was awakened by more tearing of meat, and in the dark saw a huge mass into which I fired, and was rewarded with a fairly good-sized maned lion, measuring about 9ft. 6ins. I had shot it in the chest and the bullet had gone through the heart and ended up in the hind leg! We were then worried by another lion that was getting hungry and cross and would not go away until dawn starting to break at 5.30.

A Unique Specimen

Not bad going, was it? Two lionesses and one lion in five shots and three hits, one in each. We of course did not have enough salt in camp, and to save Billiter's lioness (his first) and my lion I have had to sacrifice my lioness. I have got the claws, floating bones and skull, however. I enclose you one of the floating bones, you can be quite right in saying that it is from the first lion shot in German East Africa by any of the British troops! Last night a lion and lioness came and ate most of the remaining meat but nobody sat up for them.

There is no war news for you. We have been reinforced by 60 of the 129th Punjabis and now number 120 strong, with two Maxims. Of course, if attacked we should be reinforced in a few hours from the main body in Longido. We are a merely an outpost in force. Good-bye and good luck to both of you. – From your loving son."

It was not all fighting. Hunting for sport and the pot was an occupation undertaken by many officers and soldiers.

Left: British soldiers returning from a hunt in German East Africa.

(courtesy of Fotolibra)

Divisional staff 2nd and 3rd Brigades. There is now in Serengeti practically the whole Division consisting of:

> 1st Brigade - K.A.R., Loyal North Lancs, Rhodesians, Baluchis,
>
> 2nd Brigade – 5th, 6th, 7th and 8th South African troops,
>
> 3rd Brigade – 9th, 10th, 11th and 12th South African troops, and
>
> 2500 cavalry – armoured cars – and approximately 40 big guns.

Tuesday, March 7th

The rest of the Division arrives in Serengeti.

Wednesday, March 8th

Bombardment of Solyta from Langoro drift by the two 4-inch guns and by the new 12 pounders, the first brigade being just beyond the drift. This was more or less a bluff as Smuts and the 3rd brigade had gone with the 4-inch howitzers and the quick firing 13-pounders to take Charlo and attack Taveta tomorrow.

The Longedo force of 2000 mounted men and mountain battery has entered Ngari Nairobi, we hear, the Germans having retired to Ngari Nyuki. The force is only 25 miles from Moshi.

The caudrons wirelessed to the guns observations of their fire.

The army B.E. biplanes were only scouting. The 200 cavalry with General Van de Wenter have gone to the north of Jippe and camped there tonight. We expect a battle tomorrow as we shall probably advance on Solyta and Smuts on Taveta, the cavalry operating from the South.

I went with the staff out to where the big guns were operating on Solyta, which was all that happened this side, not a single rifle shot being fired.

Thursday, March 9th

The big guns again bombarded Solyta but no infantry advance was allowed until the evening when the K.A.R. advanced slowly through the dense bush in very open order. They found the lower trenches, guarded by barbed wire, evacuated and further on up the

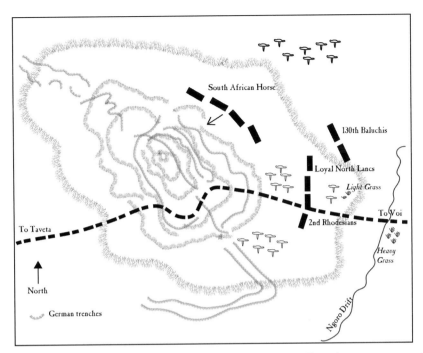

Maps detailing the Allied Advance on Salaita Hill and on to Latima Nek

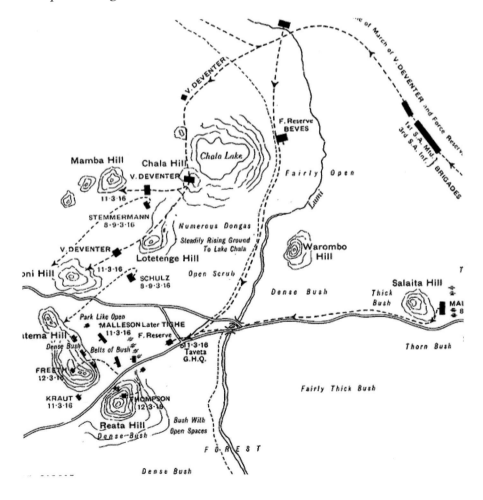

hill found the whole hill evacuated. At 10 am I had orders to take the staff engineer to Van der Wenter's column on the Lumi – a nice cheery job 15 miles across country through the bush. I got there in an hour and a half and met no Germans on the way, although when I got to camp, I was told 50 had just been seen close to the road. The camp too, and a transport column, had been attacked last night – our casualties: 4 killed and 12 wounded. Also 2 ambulances attacked and a driver shot. I found kit lying all over the road where the attack had taken place. They expected to be attacked again so I hurried back. Smuts was there joining up with Van der Wenter who was getting behind Taveta.

Friday, March 10th

Moved off from the rail-head at Langoro drift early and went right through to Taveta without any opposition where we found Smuts and 3 South African regiments who had come down from his camp up on the Lumi 3 miles above Taveta. He left a force on Charlo. Van der Wenter with cavalry is ahead somewhere between Taveta and Moshi. I had a chance to have a good look at the Sangers and dugouts on the left slope of Solyta as we passed through - which were very strong indeed. We did not get into Taveta till late at night having great trouble in crossing the Lumi – everyone getting scared as there were reports that a German force was preparing for a counter-attack as it crossed. We had a very uncomfortable night at Taveta – little rain – the General's was the only tent among the ten thousand odd troops. General Smuts was up in the old mission house. Taveta is strongly fortified with innumerable grass bandas etc. No loot or any stores seem to be left behind.

Saturday, March 11th

LATEMA HILL BATTLE

We were not attacked last night and all the transport got over the drift and into Taveta this morning. We hear the Longido column is somewhere between here and Moshi. Van de Wenter is away on the right somewhere in the Kilimanjaro foothills where he has seen a very big gun the Germans have, so we may have a hot time of it on our advance towards Moshi.

During the day Headquarters was moved right across to the other side of Taveta where the old Commissioner's house stands which the Germans had used as a hospital. There were

Ox wagons were the only means of conveying the sick for most of the campaign.

8 or 9 graves of white Germans who had died there. Two rough, rocky kopjies covered with scrub lie about 2 miles beyond this standing out on the plain and between them runs the track to Kahe to where the Germans from Taveta have retreated leaving 500 or so on these hills to cover their retreat with maxims and two 7-pounders. We shell these hills heavily all afternoon from just outside the camp. At about 3 o'clock the infantry advances but have very hard work through the bush. The fight lasted all afternoon and the whole of the night – rifle fire kept everyone in camp awake and as it got closer to camp one wondered whether the Germans would get close enough to turn their maxims on us. We had no protection and at 5.30 am we had orders to move headquarters to Taveta Hill as the Germans were supposed to be still holding the hills. They were not, however, and though practically all our force returned back to camp. It was not until 8 am that a man came down from the hill and told the few K.A.R. left that a few of the 7th South African and Rhodesians held both hills and the Germans were retreating. I happened to be out there at the time collecting abandoned kits with Newland, so we raced back to camp and Newland told Headquarters. General Smuts was out in a moment and ordered every available car to take men out to hold the hills. There was terrific pandemonium as cars of all description ran troops out over the veldt. These climbed the hills and saw the Germans (about 600) retreating in good order towards Kahe. All the guns had retired to camp so again these had to be galloped out but too late to get within effective range. I was out all that day from 5.45am to 5.30 at night with only a quarter hour in camp carting troops, water, wounded etc. and in the afternoon being detailed to the last doctor out there to try and find the remaining dead – 180 wounded and about 20 dead had been taken in. But there was still some more somewhere in the thick bush. One wandered about with one's rifle finding discarded ammunition, blankets, water bottles, etc. all over the place in the long grass. We came to the conclusion we could find no more when a 'Z' signaller officer came up to me and Lughton, who had another car behind me, and said he had found some dead. He told me he and 23 others had advanced in the night through the neck when machine guns had opened up on them. He dropped in the grass and crawled away. It was not till late in the afternoon that he had returned to the spot to find where the Germans had their guns. I motored him through the bush back to the spot and there we found 22 dead South African and Major Mainprise, our Brigade Major, all lying in an area of about 12 square yards mown down by three maxims, the emplacement of which I found about 40 yards away behind stone sangars. Most of the bodies had been stripped naked and all rifles, except one,

THE TIMES, TUESDAY, MARCH 14, 1916
Hard Fighting in East Africa
British Success
A Night Bayonet Charge
German Rear Threatened

The Press Bureau last night issued a statement giving news of a British success on the Kilimanjaro front. The Germans were driven from a very strong position at the point of a bayonet, and simultaneously an advance from the north-east was made by a strong British column in the rear of the main German position.

The following is the text of the statement:-

A telegram dated March 12 from Lieutenant General Smuts states that the action which commenced on the morning of March 11 against the German prepared positions on the Kitovo Hills west of Taveta resulted in a most obstinate struggle, which continued until midnight with wavering fortunes.

A most formidable obstacle was present by the hills, densely wooded and steep, which were held by the enemy in strong force. In the course of the engagement portions of the positions were taken and retaken several times. A final attack with the bayonet was made between 9 p.m. and midnight, and two parties, one led by Lieutenant-Colonel Freeth, of the 7th South African Infantry, and the other by Major Thompson, of the 5th South African Infantry, secured a hold which they were enabled to maintain until reinforced the following morning, when it was seen that the German native troops were streaming away towards Kahe, in a south-westerly direction.

While the engagement at Kitovo was proceeding one of General Smuts' mounted brigades was engaged in clearing the foothills north-east of Kilimanjaro of the enemy's forces, which has been cut off from their main body by the rapid British advance on March 9 and 10. Movements are in progress to beat the retreat of these isolated forces to the westward.

Simultaneously with the above actions the strong column under Major-General J.M. Stewart, C.B., from the direction of Longido, appeared on the Arusha-Moshi road in rear of the main German concentration.

The enemy in consequence is retreating southwards towards the Usambara railway. The pursuit is being continued.

Scene of the Fighting

The Kitovo Hills are five or six miles due west of Taveta, and are on both sides of the frontier line. Through them, at a height of over 3,000 ft, runs the road connecting Taveta with Moshi, the German military station on the southern slopes of Kilimanjaro. Moshi is also the most northern station on the railway to the Usambara Highlands, where are the chief European plantations in German East Africa. Kahe is a station on this line about 16 miles south-west of the Kitova Hills. The foothills to the north-east of Kilimanjaro are scored by innumerable streams and covered with a thorn scrub, but farther up the eastern side of Kilimanjaro, the Germans have constructed a good road, which branches from the main Taveta-Moshi road about five miles west of the Kitova Hills.

The column under Major-General J.M. Stewart is operating from the north-west of Kilimanjaro. Longido which was occupied by the British early this year, is a station on an isolated mountain of the same name nearly 40 miles north-west of Kilimanjaro and between it and the Magadi Lake. From Longido to the Moshi-Arusha road is 55 to 60 miles across, on the main, fairly open country, though in part brush and forest. Arusha is the German military post on the south-west side of Mount Meru and is some 40 miles west of Moshi, with which it is connected by a good road.

It is to be presumed that General Stewart's column advance through the grass uplands between Kilimanjaro and Meru, and would debouch on the road about midway between Moshi and Arusha.

had been taken. It was the most gruesome sight I ever wish to see. I took two bodies back to camp and Lughton took two. We sent out lorries to bring in the rest. The total casualties of the fight appear to be 200 wounded and 50 killed, 230 *askaris* killed and 20 missing. 20 or 30 dead Germans were found on the hill and 2 maxims and one 7-pounder abandoned.

Monday March 13th

Monday was a quiet day. More troops being sent out to the hills, and Smuts and the 2nd 23rd Brigade going along the Moshi road to the river. We hear Stewart is at Moshi and Van de Wenter has had a big fight towards Moshi somewhere. Col. Graham of the K.A.R. was killed in Sunday night's fight. The German *askaris* strip the body of all clothes as they generally do of all the dead if they have time.

Tuesday, March 14th

Also a quiet day for everyone in camp. The motor ambulances took wounded back to Mbuyuni. Latema hill was strongly picketed and all abandoned German stores etc. brought in, including one 7-pounder and maxim rifles, dynamite and ammunition etc. A column was sent to Hema river towards Moshi and is camped there. Van der Wenter has taken Moshi with practically no opposition and Stewart is out towards Arusha. The rains seem to be setting in and I hope we move from this unhealthy spot soon. All the Germans seem to have retreated to Kahe except a few wandering bands around Gippe [sic].

Wednesday, March 15th

After a very wet night, I had to go through to Mbuyuni with the A.D.C. The road is very bad and several lorries are stuck on the road. The railway, however, is being pushed through fast and is between Solyta and the Lumi. Aeroplanes were going to drop bombs on Kahe as it was reported Germans were entraining troops there – probably retreating to Tabora – but rains seem to have set in.

I hear that on the 10th, a signaller motor cyclist was shot by Germans and mutilated – head being cut off etc. – on the upper Lumi track which I had motored over on the 9th. There are undoubtedly several German *askari* bands wandering about making the bush-communication tracks very dangerous.

COLONEL BERTRAM ROBERT GRAHAM
1874 - 1916

Colonel Graham's death was a bitter blow to the K.A.R *askaris*. Cranworth wrote, "His death was a terrible loss to our force. Not only was he a most accomplished and gallant soldier but he was regarded with an almost unique devotion by the K.A.R."

Betrram Robert Graham was born in India in 1874 and served with the Queen Victoria's own Corps of Guides. He was transferred to the 3rd K.A.R. and was involved in putting down the Embu incursions in 1904. He was in Jubaland when war broke out and rushed back to Nairobi as soon as he heard the news.

A letter from Graham regarding the donation to the Christmas K.A.R. fund, reproduced by Capell, provides a hint of Graham's personality. "My dear Capell, - Very many thanks for your kind letter and a copy of the Order which go to my wife to-day. I had not written myself as the Christmas Fund idea emanated with my wife and she has been running it on her own. Hope she won't turn suffragette later! May I take the opportunity of adding to her thanks the very sincere gratitude of all ranks of the 1st, 3rd and 4th King's African Rifles, not only for the very generous gift but also for the kindly thought which prompted it. May I say I think it is one of the most charming compliments I have every known paid by British troops to their coloured brethren. May 1916 be a *fizzis* for you all."

Cranworth had met him two days before his death. A downhearted Graham confided in him that he was convinced he was going to die that day. Cranworth then bumped into him again, this time "wreathed in smiles." Apparently he said "everything is okay today and we are going to give them hell." The 3rd K.A.R. did, but Colonel Graham was killed in a hail of bullets.

BERTIE WILMOT MAINPRISE

Major Mainprise was commissioned into the Royal Engineers in 1894. He spent most of his army career in India with the Roorkee Sappers and Miners. Thanked by the Government of India for his services during the 1897 famine, he served in the Tirah Campaign in the Boxer Rebellion in China.

Mainprise arrived in East Africa, with the Imperial Service Unit, The Faridkot Sappers and Miners, a company raised by the Maharajah of Faridhot in the Punjab. He fought at Tanga and the raid on Bukoba. General Malleson selected Mainprise as Brigade-Major of the Voi Brigade.

He was on the battleground when he met the wounded commanding officer of 5th South African Infantry withdrawing his battalion. Mainprise collected a party of 130th Baluchi and charged the Nek. He, and 20 soldiers were mown down by German machine guns. Only two of the Baluchis survived. Mentioned in despatches four times, he is buried at Taveta.

Thursday, March 16th

All quiet. Had to motor through the Serengeti again from Headquarters. Road getting very muddy and a lot of lorries stuck. It is best to make one's own track through the bush.

Yesterday, 2 natives (spies sent into camp by the Germans) were caught and were being court-martialled when one tried to escape and bolted through the camp. However, the K.A.R. *askari* guarding him bowled him over with a shot through the head at his third shot. It was a wonder no one else was hurt by the other two shots. I heard today that the Germans admit that our bomb raids on Taveta accounted for 60 lives and that they always retreated to the forest in the morning and evening. Although we are in Moshi it seems General Stewart was too slow and did not cut off the Germans retreating down the line.

Friday, March 17th

Today we dropped a lot of bombs from aeroplanes on Kahe where a lot of German troops were seen. A company of K.A.R.'s went yesterday with a pioneer named Burgess to blow up the bridge on the Railway above Kahe and between there and Moshi. They found it defended strongly, however, by Germans with a machine gun. Burgess got hit in the stomach and died here the next day. A K.A.R. officer was hit in the arm so they had to return. The rain seems to have stopped for a bit and the roads are good again. We expect to move on into Moshi in a day or two. This is very hot camp and the most unhealthy place almost in British East Africa.

Saturday, March 18th

All quiet here.

Sunday March 19th

A small Scrap going on out near Himo river for the possession of 3 hills but no details yet.

Monday, March 20th

[No entry]

Opposite above: At the start of the war, before the sappers and engineers arrived, bridges were rare.

Opposite below: Donald washing off the dust in a river.

Tuesday, March 21st

Scrap still proceeding at Rest House Hill but Germans are getting away through General Stewart being so late and not holding the rail line below Kahe which would have stopped them getting their rolling stock away and retreating down the line.

Wednesday, March 22nd

For the last 2 days operations for the occupation of Kahe have been going on. Shepherd's brigade from Moshi got attacked last night in their hastily entrenched camp in the bush. Three times the Germans attacked, charging up to the trenches with bayonets but were checked each time by our machine gun fire and the Baluchis and Punjabis. Their casualties must have been heavy. We lost approx. 50 in the night attack and 250 over the other two-day operation. 150 men a day are going sick from sun and fever. Kahe is a worse place for this – very flat and in dense bush.

We captured one of the Konigsberg 4-1 guns which the Germans had to blow up as they retired. They went to Kahe and entrained for [??] down the line.

Thursday, March 23rd

A small German patrol tried to blow up a bridge somewhere between Mwatate but a premature explosion only killed two of their own *askaris*. There must be a few wandering patrols about which make all small camps and roads very dangerous. Rumours of a German column having got through and attacked Samburu but cannot get official details.

Am still worrying Cranworth to try and get me a commission in Armoured Cars or Ammunitions Column of a battery but can get nothing settled as everything is so disorganised.

Friday, March 24th

Went to Himo again. Most of the troops were returning from Kahe and the scene of the fight. General Tighe left for Voi today with a fever. It is said he is returning to India, but not under a cloud a la General Stewart. No one seems to know what is going to happen now. If the rain comes undoubtedly there will be no move for 2 months and all troops will recoup and reorganize at Himo and Moshi. Everyone, from the General downwards expects to lose his job! The only person who knows what he is doing is Smuts and that he keeps to himself. It is certainly to be a South African Campaign.

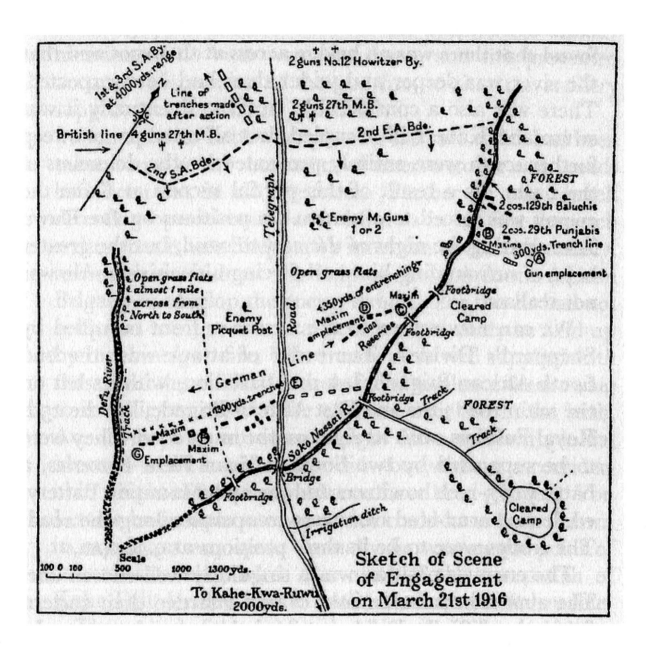

Sketch of Scene
of Engagement
on March 21st 1916

Saturday, March 25th

All quiet everywhere. Troops gradually leaving Taveta for Himo and Moshi. Over 100 men a day "go sick" with fever and dysentery and are being sent through to Voi.

It rained heavily last night and we wonder if the rains are really beginning. If so, there will be a halt for 2 months.

Britz is due up from South Africa soon with more mounted men. They are the best for this country although the horses are dying fast.

I interviewed Major Wedgewood yesterday and he hopes to get me a commission in the R.N. Armoured Cars.

The railway is well through the camp now and a siding in. Hospital trains come up daily for the sick and wounded which must be much better than the track through the bush to Mbuyuni which is frightfully bumpy and cut about now owing to the thousands of motor lorries daily using it.

Aeroplanes go off morning and evening bomb dropping, only the whereabouts of the Germans is kept very quiet.

Sunday, March 26th

All quiet and hot as blazes.

2 white Germans and 12 black brought in here this morning – surrendered.

Monday, March 27th

Nearly everyone has a fever or dysentery and as the rains are about to begin, it appears that the idea is for one Division to return to Mbuyuni and two Divisions to stay at Himo and Moshi, probably for 2 months until the rains are over.

Tuesday, Mary 28th

Taveta is the most poisonous spot it has ever been my misfortune to be in. No breeze and awfully depressing. Prisoners tell us that the Germans always had heaps of men sick here.

The Germans in East Africa

To the Editor of the Times

Sir, - A recent German note has alluded to our treatment of prisoners in East Africa. A British missionary has also recently stated that on the whole the Germans have fought cleanly in that campaign.

As one with first-hand experience of the operations in East Africa, I crave your indulgence in order to comment on those misleading statements. For many months, I suppose, I was in a position as good as anyone to arrive at the truth. I can state without hesitation that the prisoners who came in our hands were treated with the utmost humanity and indulgence. Indeed, several of the whites and nearly all the blacks, expressed their delight at being so well treated, fed, and looked after.

Now as to the clean fighting of the Germans, I state, and every one then in the fighting areas can confirm it, that on several occasions the Germans mutilated our dead, officers and men, British, Indians and Africans, in a revolting manner such as the slave soldiers of the Mahdi used to do. There were many occasions when our medical officers confidently stated that our wounded had been subsequently done to death with bayonets, knives, rifle-butts, or knobkerries. On January 1, 1916, the Germans deliberately ambushed and shot down a Red Cross ambulance car near Mzima, on the Tsavo River. As to the German treatment of our prisoners I could say much, but perhaps the following extract from a letter received by the last mail from a British Officer in East Africa will be the best method of showing how these apostles of *kultur* abide by Hague and Geneva conventions:-

"A good many of our Indian prisoners have got away from the Huns, but they still have about 120 sepoys, who are being used by porters.

"Yesterday, I was talking to an Indian officer who had escaped, and he gave the most horrible accounts of the way they had been treated while in captivity. He was a fine looking Mahomedan, and he said he was quite sure he had gone through his time of purgatory in this world, and that he had nothing more to fear.

"He looks as if he would never smile again. Soon after they were captured, the Huns took away all boots, socks, puttees, water-bottles &c., from the sepoys. Consquently the latter suffered terribly and in a short time their feet were a mass of maggots and they left a trail of blood wherever they went. In spite of this they had heavy shackles put on their ankles; these in many cases wore through to the skin and rested on bare bone. The officer mentions the case of havildar in an Indian regiment whose foot got in such a state from maggots and fetters that they allowed him to see a doctor, and eventually the whole foot rotted off and the man died. The officer also said that a German had 'Ek sipahi ke munu men pishab kiya.' The mind of a German is really beyond one's comprehension, and can only regard them as vermin. I hear they have also treated our white prisoners very badly, making them clean out the natives latrines and such like."

Sir, I suggest that it is well known that these facts should be made widely known to the British and, still more, to the Indian public. I agree with one of your correspondents in hoping that for the sake of our prestige, no Germans should ever again be allowed to possess any corner of East Africa.

I am, &c.,

January 16

Maktao

Out towards Himo, the country gets much better and healthier. Along the road there are a few coffee farms belonging to Italians, Russians, Greeks and Germans – very poor looking coffee. All the farms have been looted and everything worth taking carted off, mostly by the South African Horse.

Wednesday, March 29th

All quiet.

Thursday, March 30th

Return to Mbuyuni with the remainder of the staff. Awfully nice and cool after Taveta. Hope to get some leave.

Friday, March 31st

Units of the East African Brigade and the T.E. 7 keep on coming into camp to make up the 1st Division which is going into "winter quarters" here (Mbuyuni).

At this stage everyone naturally is fed up and depressed at the thought of two months inactivity. Britz is expected up from South Africa soon but they say he had only 2500 burghers with him.

There are approx. 8000 horses in camp here. A certain amount of horse sickness but nothing very serious. The number of horse that have died from 'fly' is not what was expected.

A GENTLEMAN'S WAR

Contemporary newspaper accounts of the East Africa Campaign contain a collection of letters and articles of the ill-treatment of British prisoners of war by the Germans. Captain Robert Dolbey, a medical officer in charge of the hospital at Handeni, wrote in his memoir, "Sketches of the East Africa Campaign" of how the Germans sent back prisoners captured at Salaita Hill "… these poor devils had been harried and kicked and cursed and ill-used by *askaris* and insulted by native porters… Kicked along the road or left to die in the bush these are the only two alternatives." However, Dolbey's book is full of vitriol for the 'Hun' and with good reason as he had been a prisoner of war for a year on the Western Front. Dr. Holtom, on the other hand, who was imprisoned in Tabora was full of complaints about his treatment. The razor he was issued was useless, the pillow too lumpy, and they were never served rice pudding!

Certainly, as in all wars, there were many atrocities and Lieutenant Henrich Naumann, during his attempt to invade British East Africa in August 1917, was believed to have been particularly brutal. He was charged with murder for his actions but was never brought to trial. However, there seemed to be an unspoken gentleman's agreement among the officer ranks. Donald mentioned that he had once spied a German European sitting on a rock well in range of his rifle. An excellent shot, he fired and intentionally missed as it was not 'gentlemanly' to pick off an officer outside of battle.

Von Lettow remarks that in the early days of the war, "the conduct of the British regular officers was invariably chivalrous and that the respect they paid us was fully reciprocated." He must have been dependent on the British sense of 'fair play'. In every town the German army evacuated the European women, children and sick were left behind to be cared for by the British.

Communication between the enemies was common. The British doctors often swapped supplies with their German counterparts. On one occasion, in the aftermath of one skirmish, a German doctor asked for the return of his medical pannier which was only done with great reluctance as it was more sophisticated than anything in the British equipment.

During the siege of Kibata, von Lettow tells how he received a letter from Jan Smuts "informing me that I had been awarded the Order for le Merite and expressed the hope that his cordial congratulations would not be unacceptable to me. I thanked him equally politely, although I at first believed that he was confusing it with the Second Class Order of the Crown with Swords, which I had received a short time before. I mention this letter as a proof of the mutual personal esteem and chivalry which existed throughout in spite of the exhausting warfare carried out by both sides."

Long after the war had ended, von Lettow sat next to Smuts at the 1929 anniversary dinner of the British East Africa Expeditionary Forces. They struck up a long-lasting friendship. Smuts sent food packages to von Lettow during the hard times after World War II and also arranged for a pension which he received until his death.

An officer of 4 K.A.R. handing over medical supplies under a flag of truce.

(courtesy of the Imperial War Museum)

"The unpleasant game is like hunting a snake in the long grass."
Angus Buchanan

APRIL 1916

Above: Governor Belfield with unidentified Staff Officers.

Opposite page: The mock-Tudor Government House.

German Defeat in East Africa, Gen. Van Deventer's Success

The Secretary of the War Office issued the following announcement last night:-

Telegraphing on April 23 Lieutenant-General Smuts reports that the troops under General Van Deventer, after defeating the enemy before Kondoa Irangi on April 19, occupied that place.

Prisoners were taken and a considerable number of casualties inflicted on the German forces, which retired in the direction of the central railway.

The action which, as the above message states, had had a victorious issue for the troops under General Van Derwenter, was actually in progress when the telegraphic report from General Smuts which appeared in The Times yesterday was dispatched. The enemy was encountered in some force near Kondoa Irangi on April 17, and General Smuts reported that it became evident that a hostile concentration was being effected in that direction.

As was stated in the The Times yesterday Kondoa Irangi, which is 100 miles from the railway running right across German East Africa from Dar-es-Salaam to Lake Tanganyika is the centre of a rich agricultural district, and roads debouch from it to all the main points of the colony.

Saturday, April 1st

General Hoskings arrived as Divisional General for the 1st Division, which is now all in camp here, consisting of: [Donald's entry stops at this point].

Sunday, April 2nd

Go to Nairobi on leave for 10 days where both Eckstein and I get bad attacks of fever which more of less lays us out for 6 weeks, the first fortnight of which I spend in hospital and then stay for a month with the Belfields at Government House.

Monday, April 3rd to Easter Monday 23rd

[No entries].

Easter Tuesday, April 24th

Am given a commission in the 2nd Battalion of the K.A.R. and told to join up on Monday next when, to commence with, one will have to do two months "on the square" with several other newly-joined officers. Eckstein obtains commission also and we are to join up together.

Wednesday, April 26th through to and including Wednesday, August 2nd

[No entries. Donald was hospitalised with malaria and then recuperated with the Belfields at Government House.]

Active service dress.

A company drawn up for inspection at the barrac

Physical drill on the parallel bars

The King's African Rifles, who are recruited from the native races, have done their duty splendidly during the war. There are, in fact, no more loyal subjects of his Majesty. There are three battalions—the Central Africa, which fought at Ashanti in 1900, the Uganda and

the East
now static
picturesq

Back view of the kit.

n seen in the pictures belong to the last-named battalion, and are
the island which we exchanged for Heligoland. They are very
are officered by Englishmen.

"They do not know what fear means; they have won the war for us in East Africa."

 A British Officer's tribute to his *askaris*

This faded newspaper cutting was preserved in Donald's copy of Lieutenant Colonel H. Moyse-Bartlett's History of the King's African Rifles.

Donald with Officers of the 1/2 K.A.R.
Dressed in field service uniform

(courtesy of the National Army Museum)

AUGUST 1916

Thursday August 3rd

Preparing to leave tomorrow for the front – 500 of us of the 1/2nd K.A.R. – 3 Companies of 3 platoons each. Nearly all the men are recruits and have done practically no field training. The same with the officers, hence a general sickness at being called to the front and split up when another 6 weeks of training would have made us a pretty good force. Personally, I have done two months "on the square" and five weeks only of training with the new recruits so have no confidence in myself or the men. Have got the best Company Commander, one Hardingham and our Colonel Soames is a most delightful person and popular with everyone.

Friday, August 4th

Parade at 12 noon and march to the military railway station – bands playing etc.

Entrain for Kongwe.

Saturday, August 5th

Breakfast at Voi and then proceed along the Taveta railway.

Sunday, August 6th

Down the German line all the tanks at every station have been destroyed by the Germans so have a many good bridges. But, in the last 6 weeks, these have all been repaired by our engineers and South African Railway Corps etc.

Arrive at Korogwe somewhere about 12 o'clock at night.

Monday August 7th

Detrain and march out to our camp about a mile and a half out of town(!) where we shall have to wait till our transport comes. We hear that the West African Regiments have already gone through, also 2 long range 4-inch guns which they hope will silence the Konigsberg 4.1 guns which are annoying the camp a lot. We are told we are to go straight to the front to join the 1st Division.

Opposite: German railways from a collection of photographs in a family album labelled "Loot from a German suitcase."

Tuesday, August 8th

We hear that our transport will be ready tomorrow so today is spent in the morning with a 3-hour parade, field training, attack a hill etc.

Very hot.

Wednesday, August 9th

Not off until tomorrow. Train.

Thursday, August 10th

March about 5 miles in the afternoon and camp in a glade by the roadside. No water or washing.

Friday, August 11th

Start off very early to do a 12-mile march. Porters very soft and keep on falling out absolutely beat. We reach a bit of rubber plantation with a good well of water. The natives say they have turned English now! and sell us eggs etc. This road was very bad with snipers about a month ago as the grass and bush is very thick on each side and a sniper could have lovely shooting at the innumerable lorries and cars running between Handeni and Korogwe. The owner of the rubber plantation was supposed to have done a lot of it so had his house burnt down a fortnight ago. All this road runs through very fertile country, very little cultivated however owing to no water.

Saturday, August 12th

Still plodding over very dusty road and one gets absolutely smothered marching in column especially when cars etc. pass one. Lots of guinea-fowl and spurfowl on the road. I did advance-guard today with my platoon and for a long way along the road there were fresh tracks of where a lion had gone the night before.

Sunday, August 13th

Started at 3.30 am and got into Handeni about 10 am. Here we are told we have to stay some time and continue training. Supplies are very hard to get forward to Lukijina – 1 tin of bully and 4 biscuits being ration for a man for about 2 days so no more troops than

Above: Colonel Soames, Colonel Bevan and the 2/2 K.A.R.

COLONEL C.T. SOAMES

Colonel Soames was a professional soldier and had fought in the Boer war with his regiment, the Royal East Kent Regiment 'the Buffs'. He was then attached to the 3rd K.A.R. In 1910 he was based in Nairobi and was in charge of putting down an unrest in Meru.

Keen on shooting and pig sticking, he was a popular personality in the small European community in East Africa and respected for his skills on the Polo field.

When he became Donald's Commanding Officer, he was suffering from a badly wounded arm, a result of the fighting to gain control of the Island of Mafia at the beginning of 1915. Mafia Island was considered an ideal base from which to track down the Konigsburg. The 1 K.A.R. managed to drive the enemy out of the entrenchments at Ngombe. It was during the fight that Soames was injured.

He died after the war on his tobacco farm in Nyasaland.

Another Soames, is listed on the Victoria Falls War Memorial in Zambia. He also served in the Buffs and was killed in France.

are absolutely necessary are sent forward. General Hannington sends 40 casualties back to Handeni today so he has had a scrap. Report says that the Germans are in a bad way in waterless bush. We hear also the Mwanza force has captured a German force.

Monday, August 14th

All *askaris* and porters are turned on to building grass huts for themselves. The water is very bad in camp, only two old wells being available for drinking purposes. This is all treated with Chlorine chlorate of lime by the doctor which gives it a horrid taste. There is a big stone fort surrounded by sisal in the middle of the camp used by the Germans as a defence against native risings. Colonel Soames is made O.C. of the camp and we are responsible for the defence of the camp etc. and have to supply about 50 men a night for picket duty besides one officer and 25 men having to picket by day and night on a high hill about 2 miles from camp.

Tuesday, August 15th

All *askaris* finish building grass huts. A very cold misty day.

We get fresh meat (of a sort?) and bread here, otherwise practically no rations. Our mess 5 of us (C company), brought 5 "chop" boxes, 2 cases of whisky and 21 cans of milk so we are doing ourselves pretty well. But, if we advance, we shall not have the transport to take these luxuries on.

The R.F.C. are about 3 miles off at a place called Nderuma. They are to advance almost at once.

The 101st Grenadiers pass through today on their way back to Kongwe en route for Egypt. They have been out here since the beginning and need a rest badly.

Hundreds of South Africans and all troops come in daily sick from dysentery and shortage of food.

Wednesday, August 16th

Sudden orders to move tomorrow to Turiani 70 miles forward.

Unidentified army camps.

Thursday, August 17th

March at 12 noon. Short march.

Friday, August 18th and Saturday, August 19th

[No entries]

Sunday, August 20th

LUKIGURA

For the last 4 days we have been marching about 10 – 14 miles a day, mostly at night, getting up at about 2 am. Nice and cool but road very dusty and every 400 yards a dead, stinking ox or horse makes one do a 50-yard run. Rather pretty country – bush and forest – but waterless and appears devoid of game. Occasionally a small village and shamba on a waterhole. One gets covered in dust which is 6 inches deep in most places and passing lorries make it worse. Lots of tsetse fly and the 6 or 8 battalion horse will undoubtedly die so will the oxen in the 15 or 30 carts we have for transport. We reach Lukigura river tonight. Very small camp in the bush with a few details and the 5th South African band which played in the evening.

Monday, August 21st

Reveille 4 am and march at 5 am. Reach Makindu 9 am (about 10 miles). Fair water. This was the camp the Germans shelled with their 4.1 Koningsberg gun from the Ngumi hills at 17000 yard range. We are to halt here today and on to Turiani tomorrow.

Tuesday, August 22nd

TURIANI

Reach Turiani at 10 am. Supposed to be the centre of the German fruit farms! We can see a few small shambas on the hill just beyond the camp and natives bring in a few pawpaws, bananas and eggs.

A good river here which, 10 days ago, the Germans were allowed to cross over with all their big guns and then burn down the bridge although they only had a very small escort

"IT'S LIKE FIGHTING IN A BALLY ZOO..."

In no way can the war in East Africa compare with the mass-slaughter of soldiers on the Western Front. Casualties from actual fighting were minimal. The real enemy in the campaign was the wild and beautiful Africa. The scarcity of potable water meant that dams, rivers and waterholes were considered valuable territorial gains. The logistics of supplying a campaign for the increasing number of troops across a lengthy and inhospitable terrain were impossible. With so many nationalities, the varied diets also had to be catered for: the Hindus would not eat beef, nor the Muslims pork and many were vegetarian. The soldiers carried a few hard biscuits and meagre pint of water with them and these rations often had to last for two days as they marched through the bush under the boiling sun. As one soldier described it: "We think of war as a matter of combats, demanding above all things physical courage. It is really a matter of fasting and thirsting, of toiling and waking; of lacking and enduring; which demands above all things moral courage."

Debilitating diseases were another natural enemy. Despite the number of soldiers sent to East Africa, the actual force fit enough to fight was small as the majority of men were hospitalised from malaria, dysentery and typhoid. The German officers, already 'salted' settlers, suffered as well but not to the same extent. It has been said that their uniforms (high necked jackets and long trousers) gave them better protection from mosquito bites.

Accounts of attacks by wildlife were unique to the East African Theatre. Official numbers record about 30 casualties from lion attacks. Donald said that at least 100 men died from lion, leopard and hyena. Emboldened by the scent of death, they graduated from scavenging the carcasses of the pack animals to becoming man-eaters. The hunter, Philip Percival's grisly story is quoted by Tony Dyer in his book "Men for All Seasons:"

> "Man-eaters are the most difficult of all lions to hunt because they have lost their taste for conventional baits and prefer human flesh. One day they found where a lion had left the legs of one of their soldiers uneaten. Someone had the bright idea of poisoning the legs with strychnine. Next morning both legs had gone and so had the man-eater."

Encounters with wild animals were frequent. It was common for elephant, buffalo and rhino to stampede through camps and giraffe were often the culprits in the destruction of communication lines. The Germans tried to solve this issue by building taller telegraph poles (the battle of Longido might never had happened if Major Kraut had received the communication with orders to move on). One would think that the animals would have kept a wide berth from the actual battles, but apparently in one skirmish, a soldier diving for cover from machine gunfire, landed on top of a surprised leopard.

It must have been soul-destroying for men like Jim Elkington, a settler who imported his own hounds, to serve in the veterinary corps. Horses, mules and livestock were as susceptible to disease as the soldiers. Most animals only lasted between three to six months before succumbing to Trypanosomiasis, transmitted by the Tsetse fly. The overpowering odour of rotting flesh from the dead animals littered outside camps is frequently referred to in many contemporary accounts of the Campaign.

and the garrison of Turiani was 70 recruits and 2 telegraphists. Our troops appear to have sat above and watched them retreat without attempting to stop them! Directly we get here we have orders to go out and join the 1st Division and not stay on line of communications.

Wednesday, August 23rd

TURIANI

We were to have left here at 4 am but orders were suddenly changed not to leave till midday.

This is a filthy camp littered with dead and stinking oxen and horses and crawling with crawlers of all descriptions so we had a bad night last night.

If we had stayed here, we are told, we should have had to go and take on the 400-600 Germans who are dug in up in the hills at the back. They will probably come down and blow up a bridge and cut the lines of communication or snipe lorries as they pass.

Saturday, August 26th

Move 9 miles down the Wami and reach there at 9 am. Rest till 4 pm and then do another 10 halting at 10 pm in the dark in bush country – general chaos. But we managed to get something to eat, put our valises on the burnt grass, and sleep just as we are in boot etc. No water. A very dry piece of country – elephant, giraffe spoor but no game otherwise along the road – a pitiful sight. Camp in a square with transport inside and pickets all around.

Sunday, August 27th

Up at 3 am and move on to the NgereNgere river 16 miles. Everyone filthy and tired. We have now done 181 miles since leaving Korogwe.

The Division left here this morning and proceeded to Morogoro which the Germans have evacuated. We shall move on and catch up the Division tomorrow.

Monday, August 28th

A short, 5-mile march along the banks of the NgereNgere.

THE CARRIER CORPS

Kariokor, a burgeoning township in Nairobi, derived its name as one of the bases of the Carrier Corps. Among the many tragedies of the First World War was the unrecorded loss of a vast number of Africans who were recruited, conscripted and press-ganged into service as the 'hands and feet' of the army. 50,000 of the 260,000 porters conscripted into this war lost their lives.

There was nothing unusual about the use of human transport in Africa. The Arab slavers used carriers in their caravans. Carrying bundles of supplies on their heads, a column of porters marching through Nairobi was the signal of a safari heading out into the bush. From the beginning of the war the Germans employed porters to carry their equipment and supplies whereas the British favoured mules, ox wagons and mechanical transport. That was until the oxen and mules kept dying and the lorries found it difficult to traverse the terrain. They then resorted to manpower.

Geoffrey Hodges in his history of the Carrier Corps, paints a sobering image:

> "The plight of the porter, with his load of over 50lbs passes imagination. Cold, wet, hungry, sick with dysentery, pneumonia or both, their only food half-cooked porridge made of mealie meal which was fermenting from being soaked, many staggering off the road to die in the reeking mud."

As the distances between the ports, railheads and the frontline increased, more and more porters were required. The porters also needed to be fed so towards the end of the war when General Northey was fighting in Northern Rhodesia, over 16,000 porters were needed to carry enough food for one day.

The sacrifices made by the Africans in the War was recognised on the Memorial to the Missing in Mombasa. Rudyard Kipling supplied the epitaph:

> "This is to the memory of the Arab and Native African troops who fought, to the Carrier Corps who were the feet and hands of the army, and to all other men who served and died for their king and country in Eastern Africa in the Great War 1914-1918".

Tuesday, August 29th

Up at 4.30 and march at 5.30, a short 7-mile march, and reach the camp where the Division has just been.

We have orders to go to into Morogoro tomorrow. The brigade we were going to is about 12 miles away near Kiroka on the Dar-es-Salaam road. Tremendous heavy artillery fire coming from that direction near Kiroka all the afternoon and we may have orders to go on at once and help the Brigade. Find Cranworth in camp here with fever. He is A.D.C. to Colonel Tancock who is O.C. of Divisional troops and to whom we now hear we are to be attached. But orders are altered and cancelled daily. Luckily we still have some food we brought down with us. We only got biscuits, mealie flour and beans given us today!

Wednesday, August 30th

MOROGORO

Arrive in Morogoro at 10.30 after a 10-mile march along very wet road. We are given a camp place in the Government gardens where we find a few limes and tomatoes left. Very fine gardens full of pineapple, citrus, pawpaw etc. trees but, of course all fruit taken off. Rather a nice town especially up under the mountain which is the residential quarter. A lot of German and Greek women about, also wounded Germans seem to be allowed to wander about from the hospital at will. We found 80 wounded Germans in hospital when we came. A lot of Indian and native shops but nothing except a little tobacco and some soap to sell. We get some potatoes off a Swiss and we shoot pigeons on the jail roof.

Thursday, August 31st

We are moved up the avenue towards the residential part. Our *askaris* get the old German police lines and we build grass bandas. I am sent out 6 miles with a fatigue party along the Dakowa road to repair a bridge which a sudden spate has washed away and find all the provisional lorries hung up there. The 1st Division, we hear, has passed Mseni Station and is on the Kisaki road. The Germans are on the hills behind us which run right back to Kisaki 40 miles off. 300 are only about three miles off at a mission and expected to raid us here at any time!

The Gurkhas [Kashimiris], their translator and Scanlan.

SEPTEMBER 1916

Friday, September 1st

Stand to arms and man trenches with whole battalion at 5 am. Trench digging and general fortifying all day.

A native comes in with report of 2 Germans and 24 *askaris* in bush about 9 miles off but Colonel decides not to round them up till tomorrow when more accurate information is obtained. More gun fire heard out Kisaki way.

Go and see Cranworth in hospital – better and hopes to get on to the Division tomorrow if there is any means of getting there.

Saturday, September 2nd

Getting rather tired of Morogoro and hope to be sent on to join our Brigade soon. The 300 Germans who were close have now moved off so there is not much danger of an attack but we man trenches every morning.

We hear that the 2/2 Battalion is marching from Korogwe on its way here.

Aeroplanes busy every day visiting Kisaki but very hard to locate Germans owing to the big range of mountains they are in.

They are using their guns to cover their retreat as they hope to get away to Mahengi or Mohoro across the Rufiji.

They blew up another 4.1 and an 8 millimetre yesterday.

Sunday, September 3rd

Build ourselves grass bandas to sleep and mess in.

Have a good look round the Government House of Morogoro, formerly a hospital, now being changed to a jail for prisoners of war!

Monday, September 4th

Battalion parades in market square and hoists the flag – royal salutes – cheers etc. etc.

Very hot and short of food. Water not too good, being full of mica.

Opposite: Morogoro Camp.

(courtesy of the Imperial War Museum)

Tuesday, September 5th

[No entry]

Wednesday, September 6th

Parade etc. Rumours we may be sent off any minute on a special job.

Thursday, September 7th

Battalion parade. No orders to move yet. We hear Dar-es-Salaam fell three days ago.

Friday, September 8th

Battalion parade 7 – 11 am.

The only rations we get issued to us now are flour or bread, meat, coffee or tea and sugar. Thank goodness we still have some tinned milk and whisky. We managed generally to 'acquire' a chicken occasionally, also a little milk and an occasional vegetable. We would give anything for jam and butter, bacon etc. etc. 6 bottles of sparkling Moselle fell into my hands yesterday! Excellent.

Saturday, September 9th

Orders to march back to Korogwe – general disgust.

Imagine it must be we are bound for Tanga, and by sea to Kilwa, or somewhere there, to get behind the Germans.

Sunday, September 10th

NGARE NGARE RIVER

6 – 8

4 – 9 am

Times, Tuesday, September 5, 1916
Dar-es-Salaam Captured
Naval Cooperation Closing round remaining Germans.

The Secretary of the War Office made the following announcement yesterday:-

Telegraphing from Zanzibar this morning the Naval Commander-in-Chief, Cape Station, announces that Dar-es-Salaam surrendered at 9 a.m. September 4. Our naval forces, in cooperation with our troops from Bagamoyo and Sadani, are now engaged in occupying the town, the former seat of Government and capital of the German Protectorate.

South of Morogoro, our pursuit of the main German forces continues. The main body of Lieutenant-General Smuts troops is about Matombo, on the east slopes of the Uluguru Mountains (south of Morogoro), smaller forces are pushing southwards through the hills, whilst to the west our mounted troops are pressing south to passages of the Great Ruaha Tiver, in cooperation with the detachment from Major-General Van Deventer's 2nd Division, which has reach Kikumi (42 miles south of Kilossa).

In the southern area Brigadier-General Northey's columns have occupied Neu Iringa, and have been directed from that point and from Lupembe towards Mahenge, in which direction al the German forces remaining in the field are endeavouring to retreat. (Neu Iringa is about 85 miles north-west of Lupembe, roughly 100 miles west-south-west of Mahenge).

Dar-es-Salaam ("The harbour of peace") has been since 1901 the official capital of German East Africa, with a population of about 1,000 Europeans and 50,000 natives. The entrance to the harbour, which is perfectly sheltered, is through a narrow opening in the palm-covered shore. There is a floating deck, and there was a wireless station, which was destroyed by the Royal Navy on the outbreak of war. A submarine cable connects the town with Zanzibar, 48 miles away to the north, and there is telegraphic communication with South Africa.

The Germans, as in the case of other places, like Tsingtau, where they intended to stay, have laid out the town in a very substantial manner, with fine buildings including the Kaiserhof and other hotels, and officers' club &c. The streets are broad and well-kept. The native town is separated from the Europeans. There is a botanic garden lighted with electric light.

Until the German occupation Dar-es-Salaam was merely an insignificant village. In 1862 Said Majid, Sultan of Zanzibar, began with a view to creating a town, to build a palace, but the scheme was abandoned on his death in 1871. In 1876 Mr. (afterwards Sir) William McKinnon began the construction, subsequently abandoned, of a road to Victor Nyanza. In 1887 the notorious Dr. Carl Peters occupied the bay in the name of the German East Africa Company. The factory which he established was repeatedly attacked by the Arabs and in 1889 he was glad to hand it over to the German Imperial Government. The railway through Morogoro to Ujiji, on Lake Tanganyika, was begun in 1905.

Monday, September 11th

BAKOWA

4 – 9 am

Tuesday, September 12th

4 – pm

Wednesday, September 13th to Sunday September 18th

[No entries]

Monday, September 19th

Very rotten with tonsillitis so stay behind in camp and catch a motor through to Handeni hospital.

Wednesday [Tuesday], September 20th

HANDENI

Very comfortable in hospital – better.

Only a clearing hospital with sometime 150 patients, sometimes 1000 lying like sardines in the tents.

Ford motor ambulance convoys come in every day and go on from here to Korogwe hospital.

Road too awful for words.

Thursday, September 21st and Friday 22nd

Rain

Saturday, September 23rd

[No entry]

Sunday, September 24th

Handeni Hospital

A German operating theatre at Handeni.
(courtesy of the Bundesarchiv)

"At Handeni, ours being a Casualty Clearing Station, our equipment included 200 stretchers with little hospital equipment, beyond the men's own blankets and their kit. No sooner did we come along and install ourselves in the abandoned German fort than the 5th South African Infantry were in action at Kangata to win 125 casualties. For us they were to nurse and keep convalescent; for there was no stationary hospital behind us, and forty miles of the worst of bad roads robbed us of the chance of transporting them to the railway.

So every afternoon I went to German planters' houses (empty of course) for forty miles around, in a swift Ford car. And back in triumph we bore bedsteads and soft mattresses that heavy German bodies so lately had impressed. Warm from the Hun, we brought them to our wounded. Down pillows, soft eiderdown quilts for painful broken legs; mattress for pain-racked bodies. And one's reward the pleasure and appreciation our men showed at these attempts to ameliorate their lot. They were so "bucked" to see us coming back at night laden with the treasures of German linen chests. It would have done your heart good to see their dirty, unwashed faces grinning at me from lace-edged pillows."

Robert Dolbey, Sketches of the East Africa Campaign

Monday, September 25th

Motor through from Handeni to Korogwe. Arrive very late and find the battalion still there.

Tuesday, September 26th

Battalion drill.

We are told we may be here four or five days before proceeding to Tanga.

Wednesday, September 27th and Thursday, September 28th

Korogwe

Friday, September 29th to Sunday October 1st

[No entries]

Above: Bogged down at Korogwe.
(courtesy of the Imperial War Museum)
Opposite page: "Three Rugbians" H.E. Belfied, F.C. Selous and C. Bulpett.

CAPTAIN FREDERICK COURTENEY SELOUS
1851 - 1917

The stories of Selous and his African adventures fuelled the imagination of young Victorian men. His books were probably the catalyst for the legions of fledgling hunters that arrived in East Africa. Officer, explorer, hunter and one of the first recognised conservationists, Frederick Courtney Selous first set foot in South Africa at the age of 20 with the ambition of becoming a professional hunter. He spent the next forty years exploring and hunting the uncharted regions of Southern Africa. He kept detailed records of the people, flora and fauna that he encountered, sending over 5000 specimens of his discoveries to the British Museum of Natural History. Noticing the depletion in wildlife, and elephants in particular, he became an active conservationist, advocating the need for controlled hunting and even had questions raised in the House of Commons.

As well as the protagonist for Rider Haggard's Allan Quartermain, Selous wrote nine books on his adventures. In 1890, he was commissioned by Cecil Rhodes to lead a column of settlers into Mashonaland. Shortly afterwards, he was honoured with a Founder's Medal by the Royal Geographical Society. Wounded in the First Matabele War in 1893, he later commanded the Bulawayo Field Force in the Second Matabele War. In 1909, he accompanied Teddy and Kermit Roosevelt on their epic hunting and specimen-collecting safari through British East Africa, Congo and Egypt. He formed a lasting friendship with the former president.

When the motley collection of the Legion of Frontiersmen, arrived in British East Africa in May 1915, they were accompanied by the aging Selous (believed to be the British Army's oldest Captain) and his butterfly net. Designated The 25th Battalion of the Royal Fusilliers, (nicknamed the Boozaliers by Grogan) these irregulars were commanded by Colonel Driscoll and included names such as Sir Northrup McMillan, the wildlife photographer, Cherry Kearton, a footman from Buckingham House, a Canadian Mounted Policeman, members of the French Foreign Legion, Texan cowboys, seal poachers and the hunters Martin Ryan, George Outram and Jock Richardson. Wild and undisciplined, they were fearless on the front line. Sent into action almost immediately, they fought at Bukoba, before marching to Moschi and through Handeni to Kissaki. Selous did manage to take time off from fighting and add to his specimen collection. Like all the soldiers, malaria took a toll on their health and their numbers. The Fusiliers were delighted when their hero, Selous, having returned to England for surgery, came back to the front with fresh recruits and the fight continued down towards the Rufiji. It was during a minor skirmish at BehoBeho that the 65-year old Selous was shot by a sniper. He died instantly. He was buried near where he fell, under a Tamarind Tree, the perfect resting place for an old hunter. In 1922, the vast area was designated a game reserve and named Selous in his honour.

Donald with the Baluchis

OCTOBER 1916

Monday, October 2nd

Left Korogwe at 8 am and reached Tanga at 1.30 – only 7 big trucks into each of which we packed 32 *askaris* and porters on top! A most glorious mess all down the line where the Huns blew up every bridge and then ran trains into each other and then burnt the lot!

Tanga is quite a good spot – well laid out and much better than Mombasa. Some of the houses have been badly knocked about by shells from our monitors and cruisers.

Fresh fish obtainable, also soda water from factory run by a Greek. We expect to be here a day or 2 until our boat "Ingoma" turns up.

Tuesday, October 3rd

TANGA

Bought a few things at the Indian shops but everything is very expensive.

A mission band plays in the evening on the front!

Wednesday, October 4th

ON BOARD INGOMA

Embark on the "Ingoma", a Harrison Rennie Liner. But we are not to steam out till tomorrow morning. A very comfortable 5600-ton boat with Indian stewards.

Rather hot quarters for the *askaris*, 700 altogether, and 7 to 800 porters, 32 officers.

Thursday, October 5th

A most comfortable, slack day on board. Spent most of the time eating, drinking, sleeping and playing cards to make up for the last 2 months.

Above: An unidentified German coastal town from a collection of photographs labelled

"Loot from a German suitcase."

Left: A photograph of a boat from the same cache.

Friday, October 6th

Reach Kilwa Kivini at 10 am but do not disembark. Load up lighters with ammunition etc.

The "Trent" comes in the same day with Admiral Crichton and General Harrington on board. There are 6 other boats in the harbour including a Portuguese cruiser and our 2nd class cruiser "Hyacinth" – the latter has done awfully good work landing marines at various places and has seen a lot of fighting.

Saturday, October 7th

Disembark in boats and lighters and go on shore. At 4 pm we march 8 miles along the road to Kilwa. We are given 1000 porters as second line transport. This makes up the battalion porters to 1900! All oxen and mules were left at Tanga.

Sunday, October 8th

KILWA

March into Kilwa. Camp about 2 miles beyond on a hill. Very brackish water to drink. Lancs encamped just by the road. 2/2 K.A.R. forward about 36 miles.

Germans sniping the road a few miles out. We are to go on the day after tomorrow.

Kilwa is a funny old Arab town with big square buildings. Very unhealthy and a bad harbour.

One monitor, "the Mersey" lying just outside.

Monday, October 9th

[No entry]

Tuesday, October 10th

12-mile march from Kilwa along a very bad track through fairly open bush country – very uninteresting – and every tree has thorns. No water. A few natives with a little quarter acre of shamba in some of the vleis which are undoubtedly very wet in the rainy season.

Disembarking from the Ingoma on to the small lighters (the ship in the distance, painted in dazzle camouflage, could be the Hyacinth).

(courtesy of Tom Lawrence).

Wednesday, October 11th

BATTLE OF KIMBARABARA

Reveille 3.15, march 4.30. 'C's Company advance guard and my platoon leading – delightful job for an amateur. Was told to expect to reach the enemy's position about 6.15. Thickish bush and small foot road through it. Have 12 scouts out in advance. Expected to be sniped at any minute. Nothing much happened until we got to within 800 yards of their position – this was 3 or 4 daub and wattle huts on a hill. 'A' Company were sent to the left and to the right while we extended and advanced on it from the front. Attacking it on 3 sides we all got along within about 200 yards of their outside trench and then fired. They replied with fire first on one company and then on another. They had snipers up the big trees and bullets were hitting the ground and zipping all round and over one. We firstly fixed bayonets and charged. The Huns ran for it down the third side into the thick bush – all except one who was not quick enough. Hardingham and I rescued him from being chivvied back down a trench by our Company who were giving him a bad time, just like a rabbit in a ditch! Total bag: one German caught in the trenches and one in a hut outside, 3 wounded but got away and one *askari* killed. We have one *askari* killed and one wounded. Thanks to their bad shooting we got off lightly. My platoon of 40 men alone used 1400. We found the Germans had good trenches and pits under the trees. Their strength was probably on 10 whites, 270 *askaris*.

Thursday, October 12th

Marched on from 4 am to 3 am, only about 12 miles really, Baluchis doing advance guard. Germans had laid an ambush with two maxims, letting vanguard pass through before they opened fire. One Baluchi killed and one captured. Both our Colonel and Baluchi Colonel had a lucky escape from ambush.

Friday, October 13th

CHUMO

Frightful lack of water in all the camps. Our column consists of 500 129th Baluchis and 600 K.A.R. and 3000 porters. Only a little muddy water in holes and always uncertain when shall find these as it is the dry time of year. We have to go so slowly scouting through

K.A.R. askari and 'Giffard's' machine gun.

all the bush and ridges on either side for ambushes. We know the Germans are only a few hours in front of us – Kibata is our objective which we have orders to take and hold till relieved. 10 hours on the march today, sometimes having to deploy through the scrub when reports of Huns about. Got into camp at 3 pm – Chumo – practically no water but plenty of coconuts. Everybody's filthy and dog-tired. Each night we have to dig in and put out pickets. Tomorrow we shall reach Kibata.

Saturday, October 14th

KIBATA

Reveille 3 am. March at 4 am. Baluchis' turn to do advance guard, thank goodness. We are told it is about 4 hours march to Kibata. There we expect to have the devil of a scrap and no information as to amount of water about. At 9 am we see the most appalling big white fort on the top of a hill about 4 hours march away. Looks impregnable to infantry without a big field gun and as if 50 men could hold off 1000! At 11 am we find water holes close to the path, a great relief as, if we fail to take this place, we can fall back on this water. After another hour's march, we find 2 wild natives who tell us the Germans all cleared out early this morning having women and children and one European in the fort. To our joy, we see a white flag hoisted and after a 2 hour climb up the side of this most awful hill we reach the fort. We can only think that it was evacuated because they thought we were bound to have big guns (as we ought to have) which would have knocked the fort down from the top of any hill. As it was we would never have taken it with infantry if 100 Germans had sat in it. The Baluchis are to return on Monday to Kilwa with the white prisoners and women. We are told to hold on until relieved and then we are to go back to Njingo and join up with the 2/2. The Germans have retired in 2 forces and are said to be in strong positions. Bag to date: 3 white Germans killed, one of them a Company OC, 3 wounded, 3 prisoners, 2 *askaris* killed, 3 or 4 prisoners. Our losses: 1 *askari* killed, 1 *askari* wounded, 1 Indian killed.

Sunday, October 15th

The first good night's sleep (in pyjamas) we have had for 5 days – did not get up till 7 o'clock, had a bath and all boys on washing clothes. Everyone resting. The last 3 days we have tried to eat some breakfast at 3 am – generally a failure! And then marching generally till 12 or 3 pm before getting any other food except some biscuits and chocolate carried in

Photograph of Kibata 1915.

*This photograph is an enigma. How it got into the family photo albums is un-
known. It shows Kibata fort without the white flag and is clearly dated 1915. At
this time Kibata was situated deep behind enemy lines so whether this is from a
daring reconnaissance mission or more captured 'loot' is unclear.*

one's haversack. This has made everyone a pretty good wreck as it has been intensely hot. Lying on one's face for 2 hours fighting at Kimbarabara gave most people a touch of sun.

Trench digging in the afternoon.

Monday, October 16th

Trench digging morning and afternoon trying to make the surrounding hills properly fortified. A company of the 40th Pathans came through from Kilwa in the afternoon with convoy of food. They report that bands of Germans are all along the road and have entered every camp as we left it to see what food was left behind. One can just see the sea, about 16 miles away from this fort. Bar that one sees nothing but this frightfully hilly, scrubby, uninteresting bamboo/elephant haunted bush/forest, an impossible country to fight or patrol in. Two spies are caught in camp and various natives come in with tales of how the Germans are burning their villages and taking their women to carry loads.

Tuesday, October 17th

"C" Company's turn to be in reserve for patrol work etc. Rumours brought in by natives that Germans are advancing to attack us.

3 pm Germans seen two miles from camp. "C" Company called on and ready in a quarter hour to march out and attack, if necessary, the approaching force.

March out 2 miles – scouts run into enemy scouts, exchange shots quite close but in thick bush. Gets late – are certain it is only an observing patrol of about 25 Germans so retire to camp where the whole force had manned the trenches.

Am warned for patrol work in the same direction tomorrow morning with Captain Hardingham – 2 platoon.

Wednesday, October 18th

Patrol out to Ponguteri 3 hours march. Scouts in front trying to search for ambushes in the thick bush. Frightfully mountainous country, places where 50 men could ambush a thousand. Very nervy work. Find Ponguteri deserted. Enemy were here last night, probably a double Company. Sent a section to Nakenyu 2 hours away – they are fired on and report 70 Germans entrenched there.

Giffard Machine Guns Company.
Perhaps the soldier standing is Lieutenant Colonel Giffard who later
provided the forward to Lieutenant Colonel Moyse-Bartlett's History of
the King's African Rifles.

Send back to camp for another platoon to reinforce us and hold Ponguteri while Hardingham and I go on. Eckstein comes out with platoon at 4 pm, too late for us to proceed, dig ourselves in and spend the night.

Thursday, October 19th

PATROL TO NAKENYU

Am sent up with my platoon to Nakenyu to ascertain enemy strength and see their position. A long day's work through poisonous country for ambushes etc.

Return by afternoon after having ascertained the enemy have gone on. They were not dug in.

Eckstein patrols along Samanga Road. All three platoons return to Kibata – very tired. I have done about 20 miles today in very hilly country and in the heat of the day.

We hear that 2/2 K.A.R. (Golworthy's Company) took on 60 Germans. Killed 8, wounded 42, captured Europeans and killed 13 *askaris*.

Friday, October 20th

KIBATA

40 L.N. Lancs came in last night with convoy of food. One man shot himself from sunstroke on the way. Have to send in a platoon of K.A.R. to escort them back.

Saturday, October 21st

KIBATA

Trench digging. 'A' Company on patrol and half 'B' Company. Various German porter deserters come in saying Germans are going north.

Sunday, October 22nd

Trench digging.

Top right: The album caption reads "Ready for action (note grass in their hats)."

Bottom right: Rifle Practice:
The K.A.R. on a training exercise.

Monday, October 23rd

'A' Company and 'B' Company return from patrol towards Ponguteri, Nakinyu and Mbongola. They all had little scraps with the enemy. Bag appears to be: one white German and one *askari* killed, one captured. We had two wounded and one missing.

Enemy are in force at Nakinyu, also on the road from Utete and we expect to be attacked here soon. Intelligence Department from Kilwa warns us of this also. Schemes for storing water in the fort going on. Trouble is our enemy would go and sit on our waterhole below fort.

Tuesday, October 24th

Big guns heard by the pickets towards the coast. Imagine it is a gun boat shelling Salanga or Kinganda.

The Colonel leaves us for Kilwa as his arm hurts him and he is not fit. General regret. Everybody trench digging etc. No news of the Germans.

Wednesday, October 25th

Hardingham, Eckstein and I sent on patrol with 3 platoon to Mwengu to reconnoitre Mombingwai – said to be strongly held by the Germans. Camped the first night on the top of a high little hill thickly covered with bamboo. Took 2 hours to dig ourselves in for the night. Patrolled both roads but found Germans had retired. Note from Boma at Kibata recalling us early tomorrow morning as we have orders to move.

Thursday, October 26th

Stand to arms in the trenches at 4.30am to 6am. Then march back to camp. Orders to move 3pm to Ntumbei-chine. Pack up, leave half 'B' Company at Kibata well dug in to garrison it.

March to Mission at Mtumbei-juu and camp the night there.

MEND AND MAKE DO

From the outset of war, only two ships managed to make it through the allied blockade. The first blockade-runner, the Kronborg, arrived on the coast in April 1915 with supplies and 1,600 tons of coal intended for the rescue of the Konigsberg. Communication over the Kronborg's mission was intercepted by the Royal Navy and the Hyacinth was sent to stop the blockade-runner. Under heavy bombardment, the Kronborg managed to make it to an inlet beyond Tanga. Before disembarking, her crew doused the decks with fuel and the boat ignited. Prevented by land-based German gunfire, from investigating the now burning and sinking boat, the Hyacinth returned to Zanzibar under the illusion that the Kronborg had been scuttled leaving nothing to salvage. However the Germans managed to recover a large amount of the weaponry, ammunition, telephone equipment and important medical supplies. The Krongborg's crew, now stranded on land, were incorporated into the army.

In March 1916, the Marie slipped into Sudi Bay near Lindi with 1500 tons of cargo including artillery, ammunition and medical supplies along with two medals for von Lettow-Vorbeck. Von Lettow-Vorbeck admitted that it was only to due to the Marie's timely arrival, that his army was able to continue the fight. He later said that the Allies greatest defeat was their failure to destroy the two blockade runners.

German ingenuity deserves to be admired. Schnee's modern research stations were devoted to inventing substitutes. Edward Paice provides a detailed list in "Tip and Run": "Candles were fashioned from beeswax, salad oil was made from pressed peanuts; soap was manufactured using charcoal or soda from Lake Natron; ships' life belts, euphorbia wood and corn cobs provided the wherewithal to make 'cork'; and kifefe, a soup of salt and beef fat favoured by many *askari*, was found to be a potent balm for ridding dogs of fleas." When currency became scarce, coins were stamped out of scrap metal.

Before the Allies moved into the Usambara Mountains and later Dar-es-Salaam, where the research institutes were based, an ersatz toothpaste, Whisky and a type of petrol had all been invented. Sisal rope dipped in rubber from the local plantations was used as replacement for bicycle tyres. Local cotton was used to weave the fabric for uniforms. Bandages were fashioned from tree bark, salt was harvested from evaporating sea water, honey was used instead of sugar and hippo fat replaced standard cooking oils. When wheat was scarce, bread was made from whatever grains came to hand or sweet potatos. When boots and shoes gave out, they were fashioned out of wild animal hides with soles made from captured saddles. The Marie brought ample supplies of quinine. This was a relief to the Germans who had been dosed up with a home-grown variety, nicknamed von Lettow schnapps and described so disgusting it was preferable to get malaria.

As Edward Paice points out, the German army had a much healthier diet than the Allies. On of one his expeditions, Thornhill entered a recently deserted German Camp "I settled down in the German Officer's comfortable easy chair, made up of bundles of grass tied together. I ordered some of the men to boil the German kettle, for I noticed on a little table before me a tin of coffee and some sugar... Upon opening the departed officers' two boxes we found in the first his spare clothing and a few knickknacks and most welcome of all, several hundred good cigarettes. The other box contained foodstuffs, amongst them a great polony sausage, two loaves of brown bread and a tin of dripping."

Friday, October 27th

Reveille 2.30am, march 3am, only 10 miles to Mtumbei – awfully hilly, rocky, precipitous country through thick bush and a few small native villages. My platoon doing rear guard – reach camp 1.15. Head of column having arrived there at 9.30! Half of the porters and 2 platoons scattered on the road, dropping their loads being attacked by swarms of bees. Camp consists of small line of waterholes in denser bush than before where this track meets larger track going to Liwale. Thought Germans will pass here and want this water – so we have entrenched here and cut bush etc. Poisonous hot place. Lots of elephant spoor.

Saturday, October 28th

Clearing and trench digging – a few natives about – report large German force at Ngarambe. Take turns to sleep with our platoons in trenches. Stand to arms at 4.30am.

Sunday, October 29th

Ditto as yesterday

Monday, October 30th

Ditto as yesterday

Tuesday, October 31st

Trench digging and general defence work on the camp.

Timbey
Chere

clearing & trench digging – a few natives
about – report large German forces at
m Ngaramba. Take turns to sleep
with our platoons in trenches. Stand to
arms 4–30. a.m

Askaris of the K.A.R.

NOVEMBER 1916

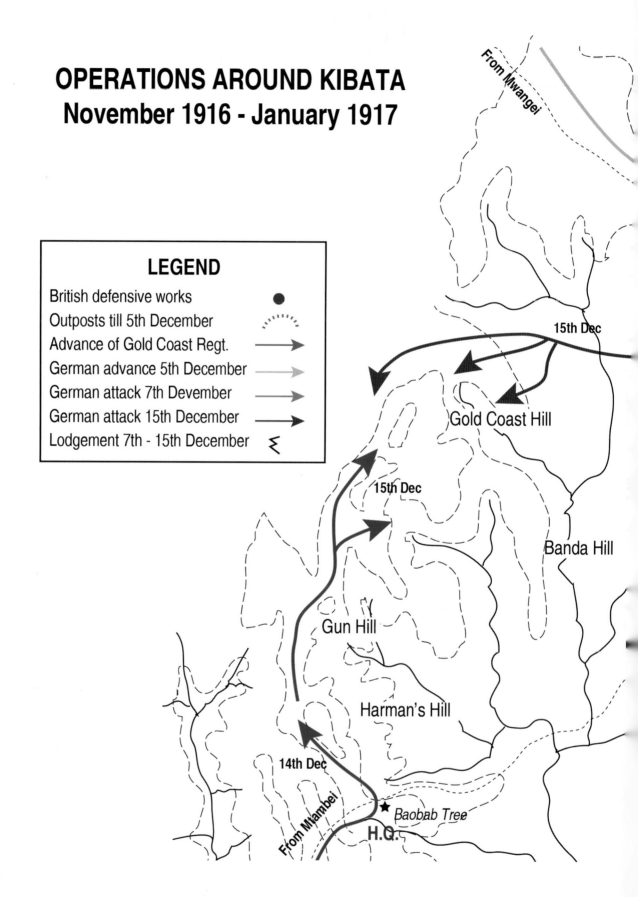

OPERATIONS AROUND KIBATA
November 1916 - January 1917

LEGEND

British defensive works ●

Outposts till 5th December

Advance of Gold Coast Regt.

German advance 5th December

German attack 7th Devember

German attack 15th December

Lodgement 7th - 15th December

From Mwangei

15th Dec

Gold Coast Hill

Banda Hill

15th Dec

Gun Hill

Harman's Hill

14th Dec

From Mtambei

★ Baobab Tree

H.Q.

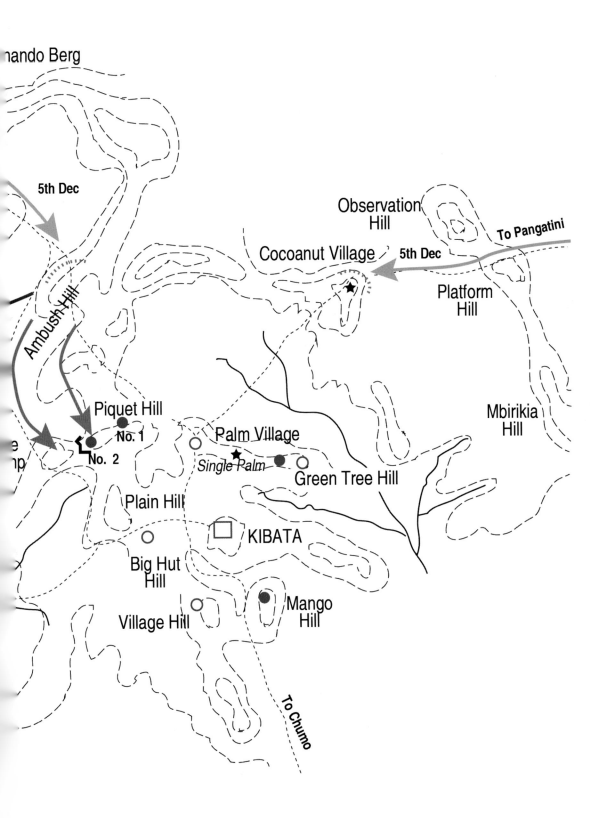

Fernando Berg

5th Dec

Ambush Hill

Observation Hill

To Pangatini

Cocoanut Village   5th Dec

Platform Hill

Piquet Hill

No. 1

No. 2

Palm Village

Single Palm

Green Tree Hill

Mbirikia Hill

Plain Hill

KIBATA

Big Hut Hill

Mango Hill

Village Hill

To Chumo

Wednesday, November 1st

Patrols go off to Nambange and Ngarambe. No native is allowed along the tracks through our camp and it is very amusing seeing them being brought in by the pickets blind-folded generally with an old puttee.

Thursday, November 2nd

'A' Company takes over defence of camp from us. 'C' Company and we go into reserve for patrols.

An 'A' Company patrol under Soames, with one platoon from Ngarambe where they captured one white German and three *askaris* escaping and another white German being out shooting. This was a supply depot – but a lot of very valuable information is acquired as a mail bag and a lot of official letters were found. They say Germans have order to advance through here and attack Nyingu on the 8th. Also they expect us to advance from Kibata on Utete! They also say Germans and Turks have seized the Suez Canal and are bombarding Aden!!!

Friday, November 3rd

Am sent out with my platoon and 50 porters to repair a piece of track from here to Mpoti on the way to Nyingu where the 2/2 K.A.R. are. They want to make it possible for ox carts to get through.

Saturday, November 4th

2 platoons, under Caldicott and Whittaker, go to Kibata by night to escort home a sick convoy which is unable to get to Kilwa the ordinary way owing to 30 or 40 Germans suddenly turning up and holding Chumo. They return late at night having done 30 miles in 20 hours. Germans all round Kibata.

Elephants all round camp to within a hundred yards of pickets.

Sunday, November 5th

NGARAMBE

Am sent off on patrol. My platoon now has only 25 men and I have to go out with three days food supply along a bush path to a crossroads where there is a big village and native

Above: A photograph of 1/2 K.A.R. entitled 'discipline.'
Below: Major Bevan and Colonel Soames with 1/2 K.A.R.

information says that there are four German whites and six to ten *askaris*. These have to be rounded up. I start off at 3 pm and march till 10 pm – a good moon. Find a lot of natives camped by the path in one place. They say that the village, Ngarambe Sulemani, has been strongly reinforced by Germans and that they have all run away. Send back report to this effect. Cheery outlook! Spend night hidden in bushes about 500 yards from path to waterhole.

Monday November 6th

Up and off as soon as it is light, 5.15am. My scouts reach big open shamba with village in it and crossroads at 7.30. Leave my platoon and creep on to have a look with my glasses. See about 400 yards off one white German sitting by doorway of grass house. Also boys about. Impossible to see how many *askaris* are there. While watching from the edge of the bushes, an *askari* walks out and comes straight towards me within 100 yards, then halts behind a big baobab tree. Refrain from shooting as wish to catch white man alive. Send a section of 10 men to try and get right round into bushes behind village. These were seen on the way and we came into pretty hot fire from the village. We opened fire and then advanced in open order – firing volleys at village on the way there seemed to have been one European and 16 *askaris*. These all ran away after we had fired 200 rounds at them and they had fired about the same amount. The shooting lasted about half an hour. No casualties on our side. I then took the village, burned all the huts and houses, brought away the German's box and blankets etc. and went back to my camp where I had left my porters etc. Stayed there till 4 and then marched back to camp getting in at 9 pm having done about 30 miles since yesterday afternoon. Eckstein had gone on a similar patrol to another place. But the Huns had heard my shooting and cleared before he got there.

Tuesday, November 7th

Much needed rest all day till 5.30 pm when general consternation owing to runner coming in saying Kibata is being attacked and we have to go to its relief at once. 15 miles on mountainous roads.

March off whole battalion 8pm leaving 100 Baluchis of 129th to guard camp.

Wednesday, November 8th

RELIEF OF KIBATA

March all night with only one hour's rest – get within a mile of Kibata just before dawn. 2 platoons of 'A' Company have to take the first two hills. This was luckily done just before it was light. We lay in the path and watched them go up. A lot of shooting for half an hour and then cries of "sekola" [?] from our *askaris*. We knew we had taken the first two hills. Kinealy, of 'A' Company, got onto the hills and found one white German with *askaris* within a few yards of him. The German shouted "We are the K.A.R.s" and then fired at him at twelve paces and missed! Kinealy did likewise! The German then ran. We advanced and took hills to the right unopposed. This gave us communication to the fort from behind. There Germans were holding two hills in front about 800 yards from the fort using all our old trenches. Could not show a head or come out into the open anywhere but they open fire with machine guns – general duel all day between the forts, machine guns and the Germans and between 'A' Company on the hill and the Germans. We were more or less left alone. Very tired and hot and hungry. Instructions for our 'C' Company to attack the German's hills at dawn! We knew it would be impregnable and after a bit this order was cancelled. General fusillade all day up to 8 pm. Another night in boots and clothes and awake most of the time – but silence after 8pm. We wonder if they have gone.

Thursday, November 9th

Careful scouting in early morning – 2 hours. Germans have retired – probably afraid of us going right round behind and cutting their communications or our machine guns also gave them a bad time in the detached post redoubt (D.P.R.).

We are sent to take over the D.P.R. and rebuild it.

Friday, November 10th

CALDICOTT AMBUSHED

Caldicott, Second-in-Command of 'C' Company, is sent out with half of 10 platoon to see which way Germans have gone. He walks into an ambush one mile from camp within 600 yards of our out picket. He has only 20 men with him. Firing lasts an hour, then I am sent to reinforce him with my platoon and take him more ammunition. I find that he had driven the enemy out of the thick forest on the hill nearly completely. We form an extended line and advance carefully to the top of the hill. A few more shots are fired and then hill seems to be clear. But one cannot see 300 yards in front of you. We find one German *askari* dead and one wounded. Caldicott has two killed, one wounded and one missing. We wait for orders and send out small patrols who find a German camp one-and-a-half hours away. The wounded man tells me there are 3 companies there. At night I am left with my platoon in forest as ambush in case the enemy return but I am recalled late at night.

Saturday, November 11th

In D.P.R. Trench digging again. Reported in evening – Mission is held by Germans and we are cut off from Kitambi. No convoys can get through.

Sunday, November 12th

Baluchis from Kitambi are supposed to be attacking the Mission while 'A' Company demonstrates up the Mahoru Road. Result: German's small force retreats.

Monday, November 13th

Trench digging. Report Germans are going to attack us tomorrow morning. They are concentrating at Mwengani – general disturbed nights which does not improve anyone's nerves.

Tuesday, November 14th

All quiet – digging like hell.

Wednesday, November 15th

Ditto

Thursday, November 16th

One of my patrols meets a German one about 2 miles out. A corporal of mine gets wounded in the head, shot at 6 yards range. The bullet hit a tree and splintered – cutting the woodwork of his rifle in three places, also his head. No patrol seems to get to Mwengai and have a look at the German position there and see the number of troops. They have so many pickets out, they always fire at our patrols. Mwengai is only three hours from here.

ALAN CALDICOTT

Alan Caldicott was only 28 when he died in the ambush. Gazetted in to the Loyal North Lancs in August 1914, he had served at the Front before being invalided home. He had only just arrived in German East Africa, having been attached to 1/ 2nd K.A.R. on 7th December 1916.

Educated at Bradfield College, he had been employed by the Imperial Tobacco Company in Blantyre in 1907. His name is listed on the War Memorial in Coventry.

We hear the Baluchis 129th are coming here tomorrow. It means, probably, we shall have to advance and do some battle fighting.

Friday, November 17th

Moved into reserve for four days. Baluchis take over perimeter.

Saturday, November 18th

Baluchis send a small patrol towards Mwengai but they did not get there as they bumped into a small German picket and had a small scrap. One Baluchi hit. The only information about Mwengai is obtained from natives and this is very indefinite as the Germans hunt all natives out of their camp and vicinity whereas we allow them in here promiscuously. Many of them are bound to be spying for the Germans. There are supposed to be 2 Companies at Mwengai well dug in on a hill and, behind them, at Mombingurai, an hour further on, another Company or two, and then another lot at Kitape

The rains are close and we ought to advance soon. We are waiting for the rest of the brigade. 'C' Company's having a good rest – everyone was jumpy having been so long on the perimeter and the week before having been fighting most days. Very very tired of the same food. Trek ox and cassava and biscuits and jam.

We are in touch with Kilwa, the headquarters from here now, but heliographing out to a small island at sea which can signal to Kilwa.

Sunday, November 19th

All quiet except for small Baluchi patrol with German picket.

Monday, November 20th

Still in reserve. Write letters.

Tuesday, November 21st

Called out hurriedly at 12 noon – 3 platoons 'C' Company to go out and try an catch a German patrol. Five whites and 50 *askaris* said to have gone towards Chumo.

Leave camp 1.30 get onto their tracks at 3.30 – run into them 6 pm. Scrap in awful long grass and bush at about 100 yard range. Eckstein wounded and one *askari*, one German

Kibata Fort with the British flag flying.

askari wounded also. Two left rifles and bandolier behind. It then took us 11 hours to get Eckstein back to camp over the most appalling rocky mountain track through bush and in the dark. Stretcher bearers did wonderfully. Reached Kibata 5 am never having had more than 10 minutes rest at any time since 2 pm yesterday.

Wednesday, November 22nd

Baluchi doctor sent for. Arrives 11.30. Operates on Eckstein satisfactorily and we hope for the best.

Thursday, November 23rd

Eckstein died 8.25pm

Friday, November 24th

Kibata

Funeral of Eckstein 8 am

'C' Company goes back to detached Post.

Saturday, November 25th

[No diary entry]

Sunday, November 26th

We hear that the Baluchi patrol that went to Kitude has captured a white German.

Big mail arrives

We now have in camp here:

500 Baluchis	1 Section Ford Ambulance
3 machine guns	Sanitary section
2 Roxxas	Telegraph Operators
600 K.A.R.	1000 porters
4 machine guns	

LUDWIG ALFRED ECKSTEIN
1893 - 1916

Eckstein's death was a huge blow to Donald. Mentioned at the very beginning of the diary, he must have been a comrade in arms and an acquaintance prior to the war – his name is listed on the Muthaiga Club members war memorial.

Born in England, Eckstein's family had strong ties with South Africa. His father, Hermann Eckstein, played an influential role in the South African gold mining industry, and was the first President of the Chamber of Mines. (After Hermann Eckstein's death, a portion of a park in Johannesburg was named in his honour). The family moved to England after the price of gold slumped.

Eckstein went to Eton and then at some point moved out to British East Africa. His brother Hermann is listed as farming in the protectorate in the 1920's and his son Anthony was a contemporary of Tony Seth-Smith at Kenton College. Donald always reminded Tony to be nice to the Eckstein boy!

After his death, Ludwig Eckstein was buried at Kilwa and later moved to the Commonwealth War Cemetery in Dar-es-Salaam. He was only 23 years old.

Monday, November 27th

Still trench digging and general fortifying of camp.

Tuesday, November 28th

We hear the Germans are bringing up to Mombingwa [?] a 4.1" gun. 300 porters to drag it and each shell takes a porter to carry it.

The Baluchis did a patrol today towards Kitunda, met 4 whites and 15 *askaris* – captured one white.

Wednesday, November 29th

We hear that Northey has captured 60 white and 200 German *askaris* – the first real good haul we have made.

One or two shots fired last night, and we hear that 5 lion killed 3 of our mules and dragged an Indian out his hut by the foot – by 'A' Company hill.

Thursday, November 30th

Was told to report on and estimate labour required for the possibility of improving the Kabata hill to Chumo track so as to be passable for pack animals.

"BEES PUT WHOLE BATTALIONS TO FLIGHT"

H.L. Pritchard, History of the Royal Corps of Engineers.

The African bee is the vicious relative of its more docile European cousins and was listed as one of the natural enemies faced by both sides. Disrupted by the noise and churned up earth, swarms from the wild and cultivated in rustic tree-log hives, often attacked the troops. At one point it was thought that von Lettow-Vorbeck had employed the use of bees as part of his weaponry. It was rumoured that they would place beehives by the side of the road, and dislodge the lids with concealed wires when the British soldiers walked by. In actual fact the Germans were just as susceptible to attacks from bees whilst they travelled through the bush.

The Battle of Tanga was nicknamed the Battle of the Bees. Disturbed by the gunfire, they attacked the 98th Infantry and the Loyal North Lancs with a vengeance. The soldiers scattered in panic and pain – some men had over a 100 stings.

Bushmen, like Thornhill, enjoyed nothing better than raiding the hives for honey. On one occasion on the Pangani river, he got his comeuppance when a hives fell out of the tree and a force of irate bees attacked him and his accomplice. Complaints of hive-raiding had already been made by the local Africans, and his arrival back in camp with a swollen face gave him away as the culprit.

Incidents of African Bush Fighting
(from our special correspondent)
Cairo, Jan 24

According to unofficial news which has reached Egypt from East Africa, the Germans with their black troops, engaged in an action at an East African port, which resulted in the withdrawal and re-embarkation of the British landing force, showed remarkable skill and resource in the bush fighting. Ropes were hidden under sand and brushwood and stretched across paths and when trodden on by our troops, brought down flags hoisted in the trees. By this means the ranges were accurately marked. The fall of the flags was the signal for a heavy fire from sharpshooters and sometimes machine guns, which had been hoisted into trees further to the rear.

Another device, which would almost seem to have been suggested by Kipling's tale of how an invading pack of 'Red Dogs' was destroyed by the 'little people,' was resorted to by the enemy with some success. Hives of wild bees partially stupefied by smoke, were placed under lids in the bush on each side of narrow tracks, along which our troops must advance, some hours before the attack began. Wires or cords, concealed in the same manner as those attached to the range-finding flags, lifted the lids when touched by the advancing troops, and swarms of infuriated bees, recovered from their temporary stupor, were let loose on the attackers. The failure of the attack at certain points is said to have been due as much to this onslaught of the 'little people,' as to the German rifles and machine guns, many men being so horribly stung in the face or hands as to be temporarily blinded or rendered incapable of holding their weapons. Over 100 stings were extracted from one of the men of the Loyal North Lancashires.

Since the bombardment of Dar-es-Salaam, the situation has improved and the hope was expressed on the East Coast that our forces will soon be able to take the offensive.

"I wish to hell I was in France. There one lives like a gentleman and dics likc a man, here one lives like a pig and dies like a dog."
From the forward to Angus Buchanan's "Three Years in Africa"

DECEMBER 1916

Friday, December 1st

The rains appear to have started – a very wet morning. We begin to wonder when the Germans from Mwengai are coming to attack us. They are supposed to have 2 4.1" guns there. Also Von Lettow-Vorbeck is supposed to be coming himself. We stand to arms every morning at 4.30am and have lots of pickets out. On the other hand, the Germans have so many pickets out on the hills that we cannot anybody get close to spy on the camp. Kibata Fort which was white, we have muddied dark so as not to make it such a good target. Also we are busy digging dugouts etc.

Saturday, December 2nd

Move into Reserve after 7 days in the detached post. Sleep in pyjamas tonight and not in boots! Also no standing to arms at 4.30am.

Small mail arrives.

Sunday, December 3rd

In reserve.

Monday, December 4th

In reserve. Rather seedy.

'B' Company sends by patrol to look at Mwengai. Huns still entrenched there.

Tuesday, December 5th

In reserve. Very seedy still.

Wednesday, December 6th

COMMENCEMENT OF SIEGE OF KIBATA

Shots fired at 6 am by our picket on a German white and 4 *askaris* who came out into the road about a half mile from camp and started spying the 2 redoubts on Detached Post Ridge. This was followed at 1 pm, when were having lunch, by a machine gun opening up on Detached Post, also by our replying. We wonder if this is the attack on Kibata so often rumoured. The bullets whizz all round the hut we are in reserve on Big Hut Hill and we have to get under the E side for shelter and hold ourselves in readiness for orders. The trouble is a convoy of porters with ammunition and barbed wire etc. is coming in from Chumo today. By 4.30 shooting is pretty general from all hills. At 5.30 my platoon is advised to go out and bring in the convoy as it has been fired upon and most of the porters have thrown down their loads and run away. However, I meet most of it a mile from camp and bring it in safely. I then go in reserve to the fort with No. 10 platoon. Caldicott and No. 9 go to Detached Post Ridge 2 and Wilson to Palm village. A fairly quiet night till 8am this morning when they start shelling the fort. We sit tight in a dugout and not a great deal of damage is done. They are shelling the fort with a 4.1" and No. 2 redoubt with a 15-pounder.

Thursday, December 7th

At 5.30 I am told to rush my platoon up to Detached Post as the Germans are almost through. A 10-minute spring through bullets and several shells get one there. I find the attack dying down but it is impossible to lift one's head above the parapet. I find Caldicott has been killed. Smith of the Baluchis is wounded while I was talking to him and in No. 2 redoubt most of the parapets are blown down and trenches full of dead Baluchis - 8 killed and 33 wounded out of the 60! I have to relieve them with my platoon till 8 o'clock when Hardingham comes up with another platoon. We clear the trenches and dig all night to get more barbed wire up, only lying down for about half an hour. Expect attack at dawn.

Friday, December 8th

They do not in fact start shelling again until 8 am. The only thing is to lie flat in the trench. Several shells burst within a few yards – fumes very bad – men got rather shaken – general machine shooting hill to hill all day. I am relieved at 11.30am by Longworth of 'C' Company who arrived two nights ago. Not much doing except heavy machine gun fire on both sides and periodical shelling of fort and redoubt. Sleep in reserve between the 2 redoubts on ridge tonight. Still very seedy and, what with no proper meals and never taking off equipment, one is nearly done.

Saturday, December 9th

Last night we find the Germans have got up within 150 yards of No. 2 redoubt and have dug themselves in. So attack is made tonight along ridge by Baluchis and K.A.R.s – only

150 yards – but found Germans too strong – nearly all white men in trench so we have to retire with loss of about 20 men and Captain Browning. All our K.A.R.s are getting very shaken now and I had a great job to get my men to stand up and take over the parapet. We are relieved at about 1 am and go back into reserve in the valley. The 2/2 K.A.R.s who relieve us arrived last night having done a lot of forced marching. Casualties over the last 4 days are about 150 and 500 shells have been fired into camp.

The 27th M. Battalion arrived with the 2/2 and have been firing at Hun trench which is now being sapped-up close to our No. 2 redoubt. We can hear them talking and digging by night and we, on our side, run out barbed wire between obstacles and parapet.

Get a good sleep tonight in spite of a few shells dropped in by night.

Sunday, December 10th

The enemy brought a big gun up close in the night and knocked out our M.S. in No. 1 redoubt killing Bryant and burying the team. Heavy shelling all day. Goldsworthy wounded – ankle shattered by portion of shell.

Monday, December 11th

'C' Company take over Village Hill, Mango Hill and Big Hut Hill. I have Mango Hill, 2 tiny redoubts joined together by a 20-yard communication trench which enlarges into a sleeping dugout, 5 x 20 feet. I only get about a 15-yard field from the redoubt. Then comes dense bush. Here I dig rifle pits and get most of my platoon out into them as we should be shelled out in about two minutes.

Have to dig all night as trenches are very bad.

Tuesday, December 12th

8 am three German machine guns have got round into bush on our E and give relief valley and our hill the devil of a strafing until five of our guns shut them up. My scouts report enemy advancing on my hill through bush. A note to HQ brings me reinforcements – extend along bush – standing to arms all day. Dig at night.

Kibata Fort.

Wednesday, December 13th

Fairly quiet – cannot leave trenches. Am given one machine gun and Baluchi section – have to dig trenches for them at night. West African and Pathans are round by Mission to attack Germans.

Shelling our redoubts etc.

General O'Grady arrives.

Great shortage of food; water only obtainable by night.

Thursday, December 14th

Getting very tired of Mango Hill all alone with a platoon and one Baluchi machine gun section. See no other white officer although within 400 yards of next redoubt. Moon does not rise till late so cannot dig till 11 pm which means sitting in absolute darkness from 6 to 11. Food very scarce. My boy dodges about after dark and brings me some from Hardingham's dugout.

Friday, December 15th

Usual shelling and machine gun fire. At 11 pm we attack the lodgement from No. 2 redoubt – Baluchis and Lancs with bombs, Pathans shell fire from guns and machine guns. Rush it at 11 pm with success. About 6 white Germans and 10 *askaris* killed. We have one killed and 23 wounded. Find great trenches and tunnels etc. all within 100 yards of our redoubt. I am on Big Hut Hill where the forward Observation Officer is, and together we watch it over the parapet. Plenty of bullets about. My pickets run away and hide in communication trench. Have only 20 men to hold hill - all very shaky. HQ sends me message that enemy is in the valley in front and to keep eyes open. Inform them that I cannot hold hill with only 20 men. Am sent 20 Baluchis who arrive at 1 am. Enemy do not attack. Trenches full of water and very shallow.

Saturday, December 16th

As we now hold all Detached Post Ridge, the Germans can shell it with safety which they proceed to do. In the Lodgement, or No. 3 redoubt as it is now called, a Lancs officer is hit. Anderson and another officer of the Lancs get him down on the safe slope of the hill with

Kibata Fort showing the damage from constant shelling.

stretcher bearers when a shrapnel bursts right over them wounding Anderson and Lancs Officer – all the stretcher bearers blotted. Sniping going all on day.

I hear the Gold Coast Regiment, in yesterday's battle had 145 casualties out of 295 men – 29 of them officers. The Germans got a cross machine gun fire on the bare ridges they had to cross, also Howitzer fire.

Sunday, December 17th

Quiet day except for incessant machine duels between the Germans on Ambush hill and our machine guns at the fort and Detached Post. A few shells thrown at the fort bring down clouds of dust and stones. At last we are taken from the firing line and told we are to have 48 hours in the reserve valley which means sleeping in a little damp hole. But at last one gets a good night's sleep with one's boots off – having had them on for ten days and nights with only two quick changes of socks. I managed to get a hot mud-and-water bath also, and change clothes. As all trenches are full of mud and water, one is absolutely stiff with mud.

Gun battery spots a German M.G. about 700 yards off in the evening and soon removes it with a few shells.

Monday, December 18th

After a quiet breakfast, I am trying to write up this diary for the last 10 days. The General (O'Grady) has just looked in and while talking to him a shell has burst again about 20 yards off! Now another 15 yards off right in amongst the men and porters but seemingly no one damaged. If another comes close I shall have to retire to my dugout.

(Later). A fairly quiet day on the whole. A lot of shelling, most of which came about 50 yards off round the corner of the valley and all round a hut where we had just put 6 cases of dynamite. The 2/2 were to have tried to take Observation Hill, but their guide led them wrong. They had a small scrap with a picket. Otherwise things are much in the same position. Perpetual machine gun fire into camp makes it impossible to move about in the daytime.

A close up view of the neat hole made from a German shell.

Tuesday, December 19th

Another quiet night in reserve. K.A.R. casualties up to date are roughly 1 British officer, 10 *askaris* kill[ed], 4 British Officers wounded and 37 *askari* of which half are from 'C' Company. Baluchis must have had 80 casualties out of 250. WA77, 150 out of 300. Various Lancs Officers and men and numerous porters and stretcher bearers.

Wednesday, December 20th

KIBATA WATER HOLES

We are sent down to the Kibata water holes for 3 days complete rest as 'C' Company has had the roughest times of any company of the battalion.

The CO informs me that he has mentioned me very highly in his dispatches which is very pleasing.

Thursday, December 21st

CHUMO

No rest. 11 am we are sent off to garrison Chumo. Germans in that neighbourhood. 4 hours very hot march.

In spite of patrol work, it means that it was very nice to get away from the shells!

Friday, December 22nd

PATROL

After a quiet morning meeting many friends etc., at 11.30 news comes in small enemy patrol close by – probably 1 white and 2 *askaris*. Am immediately rushed out with my platoon and after a 4-hour march meet enemy on tiny forest track. They bolt. Some of my men go after him – several shots fired – capture their porter and all kit – white man not! Hotly pursued by my scouts, they have 2 miles through forest and then are lost! He had evidently been spying the camp quite close. Dine with A.C. Hoey.

ARTHUR CECIL HOEY
1883 - 1956

Arthur Cecil Hoey is generally relegated to a cameo in most of the biographies about East Africa. He began his adventurous life in South Africa where he fought in the Boer War. After a short stint working in South Africa, Hoey and his younger brother Will are purported to have walked up from South Africa in 1904 to join their older brother in East Africa. Hoey then travelled on foot to Mt Elgon and was perhaps the first white man to reach the Uashin Gishu plateau, where he later settled. One day, sitting on Sergoit Rock, he saw what he thought was smoke from a bush fire. It turned out to be a column of the first Boertrekkers on their way to Eldoret. By 1910 Hoey was well-established on the Uasin Gishu plateau. As well as growing wheat and coffee, he owned Sergoit Store, where Martin Seth-Smith would have reprovisioned during his trip in 1908. Judging from Martin's photographs, they clearly went on safari together. Cecil Hoey also accompanied the surveyors into the newly named Trans-Nzoia area where, as well as acting as estate agent, he invested in more land including a farm in partnership with Denys Finch Hatton. The town, Moi's Bridge, was once known as 'Hoey's Bridge.' Supposedly the first bridge was a simple tree trunk, felled by Hoey, so his wagons crossed the Nzoia River. It opened up access to the Trans-Nzoia District and a trading settlement soon sprang up nearby.

Regarded by Philip Percival as one of four great white hunters of the era (his list included Bill Judd, Alan Black and R.J. Cunninghame), Hoey began his hunting career on the grey side of the law, poaching ivory. In 1908, he was engaged as a hunter by the American writer and preacher, W.S. Rainsford, for his expertise in both lion hunting and knowledge of the N'dorobo tribe in the Cherangani Hills. Following his year hunting with Rainsford, he then went on a astrological survey with N.C. Cockburn, which was later published by the Royal Geographical Society. The expedition travelled through the Northern Frontier District, beyond Lake Rudolph up the Omo River and into Abyssinia.

In 1914, he and his new wife arrived in Mombasa the day before the war broke out. Hoey immediately joined the E.A.M.R. By 1916, he was in charge of the mule wagons supplying ammunition and supplies to the front line. He appears to have served in administration when Donald met him for dinner.

Well-respected in the settler community Hoey played an active role in local affairs throughout his life. He was appointed to the Legislative Council of the East African Protectorate (Legco) War Committee in 1916 and later served as the Commissioner on the Land Tenure Commission. After losing his seat in the elections, he stepped away from politics but remained on a number of councils. In 1938 as Chairman of the Game Policy Committee, he oversaw Mervyn Cowie's establishment of the National Parks.

Described as a big muscular man, Elspeth Huxely found him rather slow of speech, with a quiet humour and strong fixed opinions. He was portrayed by the Earl of Portsmouth in 1948 as "salty and life loving." Suffering from heart problems, he and his wife, Gladys, moved from the high altitude to the coast where he died in 1958.

From Martin's album: A.C. Hoey in pyjamas, on the left, on the way to Turkana.

Saturday, December 23rd

CHUMO

Rest in camp.

A perfectly impossible camp to defend – some decided, if attacked, to go out onto the hill to take them on there.

Sunday, December 24th

CHUMO

Col. Gifford with General O'Grady come to have a look from Kibata. Lunch with us. General has given up sleeping in Kibata Fort. Last shell killed and wounded 4 or 5 of his personal boys in the next room to his. Perfectly mad to stay there considering about 20 shells have hit the fort or burst inside it.

Monday, December 25th

CHUMO

All quiet except for lions killing 7 oxen last night.

Tuesday, December 26th

CHUMO

Wrote a lot of letters. Can hear the Huns intermittently shelling Kibata. Received orders to return to Kibata tomorrow. This means more fighting. I suppose, and we thought we were going to have at least a fortnight's rest.

However, anything to get the show ended or something to happen. I am not sure that sitting in camp brooding over one's troubles is not worse than fighting. We are all jealous of the wounded and would like a 'cushy' one ourselves.

Wednesday, December 27th

KIBATA

March back to Kibata in the afternoon. Heavy rain. Several German patrols about. Hear Jock Sterling died 2 days ago. Fell in a hole with a sharp bamboo spike which penetrated his leg.

SOUVENIRS OF WAR

Among the war mementoes saved by Donald is an innocuous silver fork. The still sharp knife has been carefully welded in place of one of the tines. It raises a few questions: why did Donald need an all-in-one knife and fork and why did he keep it? Perhaps it was more booty from a German officer?

A collection of bank notes including Portuguese colonial currency and a Deutsch Osta Afrika rupee are part of the collection, along with a mass of Tabora Hellers, the coins fabricated by the Germans from scrap metal including British cartridge casings.

An early version of Swiss army knife still lives in his old desk drawer. Of South African Boer War origin, perhaps it came off of the South African soldiers.

Among the prized possessions is the pristine brass gift box, complete with the Christmas message from Princess Mary, the Patron of the Sailors and Soldiers Christmas Fund. Issued as a Christmas gift from a grateful nation, the box would have contained a pipe, lighter, one ounce of tobacco and 20 cigarettes (and for non-smokers, a cartridge case bullet pencil, a silver bullet and a packet of sweets). When Donald (or perhaps Martin) received this is unknown as it often took years for the boxes to reach their recipients.

Pocket Knife from the Anglo-Boer War
Tools include pull through hook, tin opener, shot gun cartridge extractor and hoof pick.

Thursday, December 28th

Only 2 shells fired into camp last night.

Out Company for the trenches – 5 days – everything full of water and working parties digging every night. Rats very bad in dugouts.

Friday, December 29th

Getting nervous about the roof of my dugout which looks as if it would like to collapse with the weight of mud on it which drips through on to everything – digging and making bamboo hurdles for revetting. No news on German movements. We seem to be waiting for the Brigade which is crossing the Rufiji and coming to the back of our Huns from behind. It means, I suppose, they will push more this way and attack us again. One cannot move about in camp owing to their machine guns trained on it and movements at night – very dark and wet – awful.

Saturday, December 30th

Intelligence reports state that when the Portuguese crossed the Rovuma, they were attacked by the Germans who took 200 horses, 1,000 cases provisions, 100,000 rounds of ammunition, 17 machine guns and 4 big guns – so much for their help!

Heaton of 'B' Company has gone off his head – that is 20 officers out of action now out of about 80. Casualties about 400.

Germans turning their attention with their guns to Hannington's Brigade which is about 4 miles off. They landed one shell within 2 feet of a W.A. 77 12-pounder gun but did not damage.

Only about 6 shells into Kibata today, one of which landed right into my platoon pickets but did not explode.

Sunday, December 31st

Rev. Cobham holds Communion Service in "Supplies" store. Take over trenches of Single Palm Tree Hill with my platoon at 7 pm.

THE REVEREND ELIJAH COBHAM
1880 - 1917

Religion is a topic rarely covered in the histories of this war. Apart from a small chapter on Army Chaplains in Dolbey's "Sketches of the East African Campaign," there is little reference as to how the army dealt with the vast number of different faiths in such a disparate army.

There is very little information on Elijah Cobham. He is listed on the Emmanuel College Roll of Honour at Cambridge and later recorded as the vicar of All Saints, Fishponds, in Bristol. Having been sent to East Africa by the Church and Continental Society, he served as a chaplain in Nakuru in 1913 and was one of the early volunteers to enlist in the East African Rifles on 5th August 1914.

From an account in Thornhill, he was a very popular man.

> "…[he] preached to us on a Sunday in a way we best understood, did duties of a corporal during the weekdays and was able to take his place in the ring when there was a boxing tournament on. Neither was he too uppish to join in a camp sing-song… quite a youngster and the whitest man in the war."

At some point Cobham was transferred to the Chaplains Department and made battalion Padre to the 2/2 K.A.R. After Donald mentioned him taking the service at Kibata, Cobham and his battalion continued on to Kilwa and down further South, encountering the enemy in some vicious skirmishes. During a lull in the battle of Mihambia, Cobham assisted in the rescue of the wounded. It appears that the Germans held their fire while he carried Major Green but on his subsequent attempts to bring back wounded *askari*, the Germans resumed their assault. Cobham was shot and died from his wounds on 9th September 1917. He was awarded the Military Cross. The citation read, "He met his death in attempting to bring in wounded under heavy fire. He had already rescued two men and was shot whilst bringing in a third. An officer who exercised a great power for good over all ranks, and one who could ill be spared."

He is buried in the Commonwealth War Cemetery in Dar-es-Salaam.

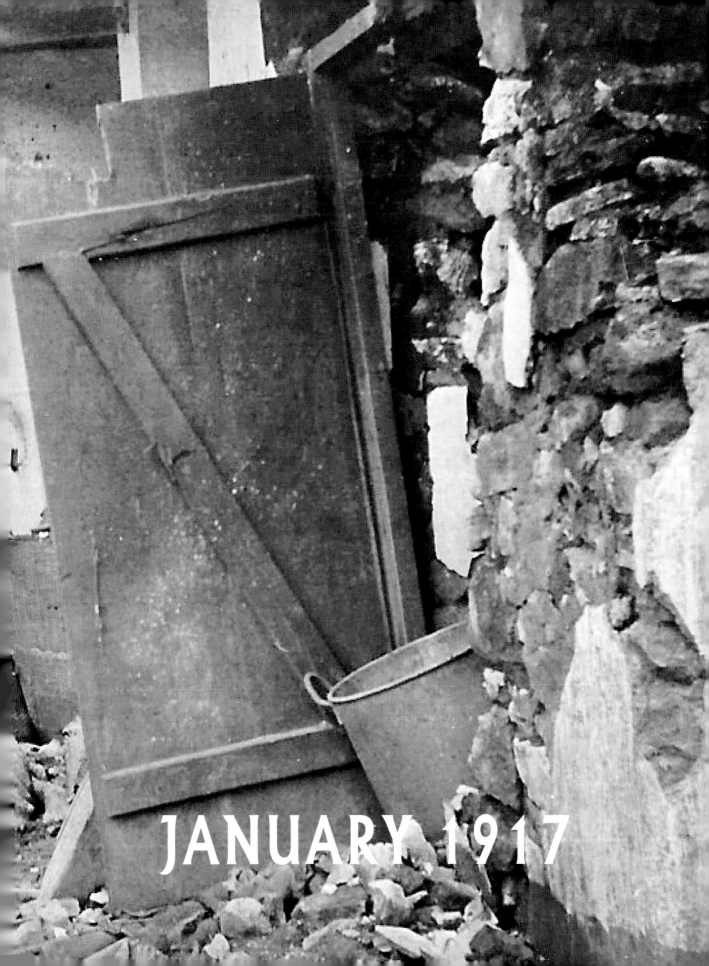

JANUARY 1917

Monday, January 1st

See big working parties of Germans 200 yards off. Telephone Brigade Headquarters and get the battery onto them. Trench digging at night 6.30 pm to midnight.

Tuesday, January 2nd

General O'Grady and Col. Gifford come to my redoubt at 8 am and while inspecting get shot at by machine gun. Spot gun in bushes at 1100 yards turn on M.B. also my machine gun here. Also see Germans digging on hill 1500 yards off. 1/3 K.A.R. 200 rifles 21 M.B., go reconnoiter Ponguteni.

Wednesday, January 3rd

Do a lot of sniping at Germans with maxim at 1100-yard range. Can see them periodically move in their trenches. They shell the fort and Palm Village but not much damage done. German 5" Howitzer arrives but ammunition not here yet. We hear General Deventer has crossed the Rufiji. Various patrol scraps but nothing of importance. Enemy seen digging in various fresh hills close. After three days and nights in trenches alone, am relieved tonight by 3rd Battalion – then for boots off and a bath!

Thursday, January 4th

Receive letter from Adjutant stating that C.O. has recommended me for the Military Cross to the G.O.C.

> "The C.O. directs me to inform that he has submitted your name to the G.O.C. for the award of the Military Cross, the recommendation being as follows:
>
> 'When the men of his platoon were badly shaken by shell fire on Picket Hill, Kabata, and about to break, by his courage and example, materially assisted to rally the men and save the situation when the enemy, under cover of his bombardment, had reached our wire.'
>
> I personally add my best congratulation on the above."

Signed

J.S. Murray

Capt. and Adjutant

To D.F. Seth Smith,   Copy.
1/2nd K.A. Rifles
4.1.17

The C.O. directs me to inform
you that he has submitted your
name to the G.O.C. for award
of the Military Cross, the
recommendation being as under.

"When the men of his platoon
were badly shaken by
shell-fire on Picquet Hill,
                    Kibata

and about to break, by
his courage & example
materially assisted to rally
his men & save the situation
when the enemy under cover of his
bombardment had reached our wire."
I personally add my best congratulations to
the above. Cp Murray. Capt. & Adjt. 1/2nd K.A.R.

1/2 K.A.R.

Rest in "Relief Valley". 2 accidents yesterday: A sentry shot his own Sergeant dead when visiting pickets and a recruit had a look at a bomb. He pulled out the pin, heard it fizz so put it back in the box. Result – 100 wounded. Heaton of 'B' Company nerves gone – attempts to shoot himself.

Friday, January 5th

Heaton of 'B' Company died this morning – Funeral 6.30. This is the 21st Officer casualty since the beginning of Kibata Battle. Howitzers shells Coconut Village.

Saturday, January 6th

Have to sit on Lodgement and spy Mwengai Road with telescope. Nothing much doing except machine gun work and sniping on both sides. 'A' and 'B' Companies and 4 machine guns are to attack Observation Hill tomorrow morning. 'C' Company and 150 Baluchis are to attack Coconut Village – most unpleasant.

Sunday, January 7th

Bombardment a success. Capture one white German.

Monday, January 8th – Thursday, January 11th

Attack Command Post etc. and Mwengai – drive Germans back. My platoon ambushed. One killed, one wounded.

Friday, January 12th – Sunday, January 14th

Rest in camp in the morning. Baluchis take Mwengai and Mambuyuni [?]

Monday, January 15th

[No diary entry.]

THE HUNGRY WAR

The old Swahili saying "when the elephants fight, it is the grass that suffers injury" was an appropriate description of the devastation left behind by the war in German East Africa.

In the words of one German Schutztruppe soldier:

> "Behind us we leave destroyed fields… and famine for the time to come. We are no longer ambassadors of culture, we are bringing death, pillaging and empty villages."

Living off the land wherever they went, the Germans requisitioned crops and livestock from the villages they passed through. The effect of this was to have far-reaching consequences. Not only was there a lack of labour with the men being taken away as porters, there was a huge hike in the price of seed and food. These difficulties were compounded by the weather: in some areas there was flooding and in others the rain failed. In 1917, the resulting famine killed off one-fifth of the population. Thornhill records visiting villages filled with emaciated walking skeletons. As a result, it is estimated that some 300,000 people, excluding those conscripted into the war, died in German East Africa and the surrounding areas.

After the war the situation deteriorated further. Spanish influenza arrived in Eastern Africa and spread rapidly through the routes travelled by both armies. By the time the epidemic ended a few months later, an estimated 2 million people had died in sub-Saharan Africa.

Tuesday, January 16th – May 7th

[During this period Donald is ill and goes on to relate:]

Go into hospital with dysentery – kept 10 or 12 days in Kibata and then sent down to Kilwa – 3 days carried on stretcher by natives – paths very wet and slippery so am nearly dropped two or three times. Only very rough damp grass huts to lie in at night with an Indian orderly to look after me – organisation very bad in this respect. Kilwa hospital fairly good but find I have just missed the hospital trip "SS Gascon" which was in three days ago and so have three weeks at Kilwa. A German medical report found states that nothing could make Kilwa fit for white habitation – hence we have a base hospital there. I leave Kilwa about February 26th on the "Gascon". We touch at Dar-es-Salaam and Tanga and reach Mombasa on March 4th. One night in hospital there and then I am sent to Nairobi, to No. 3 British General Hospital – from there to K.A.R. Convalescent Home. After 3 days there I go down with fever – temperature 104 so back I am sent to No. 3 British General for another week. Then back to K.A.R. Home for another three weeks.

Middle of April I am boarded by three doctors and told I shall be given a fortnight's leave on the farm and then am to return to Battalion. Return May 2nd – still seedy – put myself in Dr. Burkitt's hands who says I still have dysentery – obtain a week's leave from Commandant. Start on light duty at Depot on May 7th.

Porters carrying a sick white soldier in a stretcher.

(courtesy of the Imperial War Museum)

DR. ROLAND W. BURKITT

1872 - 1946

One of the most eccentric characters in early Kenya was Dr. Roland Burkitt. He was described by Elspeth Huxley as "Nairobi's best-known, best-loved and at times most dreaded doctor," Renowned for his rough and ready ways, he was nicknamed Kill-or-Cure Burkitt for his extreme treatment for malaria. For high fever, he recommended a strict regime of cold water – even babies were not spared. Many a servant was put on watch for his arrival so that his patient could escape from a comfortable bed back into an icy bath. On one infamous occasion, he drove a naked female patient in the back of his open Ford to hospital in Nairobi. As her temperature dropped, he wrapped her in items of his own clothing and so the story goes, by the time he reached Nairobi, she was fully dressed and he was naked. Sometimes a patient would get in his car and find the seat taken up by a dead animal, shot for the pot.

He kept his own strict routine and rose early every morning. Wrapped up in a dressing gown over his pyjamas, he would study the Bible or scientific journals. If he had to answer an urgent call from a patient, he went out in the same outfit, topped by a sun helmet. He loved nature and had a fixation with snakes, once serving an unsuspecting guest puff adder for dinner.

Burkitt originally came from Ireland. A surgeon by training, he arrived in Nairobi, from India, in 1911. For many years he was the only private general practitioner and was President of the East Africa British Medical Association.

A dedicated doctor, he held a surgery for the European population in the morning and spent his afternoons seeing African, including Masai, patients. On occasion he would even stretch to treating horses and believed that his cold-water treatment could bring down the fever from horse sickness.

He returned to Ireland in 1938 where he died. In a strange circle of fate, the third generation of Seth-Smiths now live in the very same house that Roland Burkitt built in Nairobi.

Convalescing in Nairobi

MAY 1917

May 7th to May 16th

Am seedy and Doctors state I have a gastric ulcer so am returned to K.A.R. Convalescent Home.

Such is the incompetence of the medical officers out here, they are all afraid of the D.M.S. who appear to be ignorant and impossible. Every subordinate is afraid of making a fuss about a patient in case he (the M.O.) makes himself unpopular and loses his chance of getting another star or gets sent back to the front. None of them cares in the least whether an officer is really ill or not. Their one ambition is to get them back to the front.

May 17th

All this time, the heavy rains have been on and everything in flood. All available troops have been withdrawn to the various bases so as to simplify transport of provisions. Enemy have been very active around Kilwa and Lindi – quite big scraps with 1/2 and 2/2 Battalion K.A.R. 150 casualties in one and 70 on each side in the other. We hear they expect another munition and store boat in from Germany, so they are probably trying to open a port.

When the new Battalions of K.A.R. are all formed, there will be 22 Battalions which will mean about 30,000 men with 600 officers.

The sickness is of course terrible – every officer of most Battalions having had fever, or dysentery or been wounded. The same with the *askaris* except those drawn from Nyasaland who seem to stand it better.

The German force is now estimated at about 900 whites and 9,000 *askaris* – and there are all their best Companies.

They have about 40 big guns, heaps of machine guns and ammunition, but must be short of food and full of sickness. The Portuguese so far have supplied them with both munitions and stores as they were heavily defeated when they crossed the Rovuma.

We are supposed to be going to advance in the middle of June about 7 Columns of 5,000 each: there will be 5,000 Belgians; a Brigade from South Africa; 2 or 3 Regiments from India; Nigerians; Gold Coast Regiment; 11 or 12 Battalions of K.A.R.s; Mountain Batteries from India; 2 or 3 4.7" guns; sea planes and on the coast area and aeroplanes. We

Above: The possible K.A.R. Nursing home that Donald was sent to. Several nursing homes were set up including one at Muthaiga Club.

Photographs from the nursing home. Kitty Llewellyn is on the left.

hope that this force in three or four months will finish the campaign which Smuts says he has practically finished!!

No news has been lately of the German raiders which were up the coast – we had two or three ships out looking for them and we heard that a Japanese Cruiser Squadron was out. Zanzibar was put into a state of defence and all the coast towns had to put out their lights at night. The other day the enemy actually brought down a mountain gun down close to Kilwa and shelled the shipping there. They certainly have got heaps of pluck and initiative. If we had only got their organisation, we would have finished the campaign long ago. One thing we are pleased at is that two or three Germans have been shot and others imprisoned for their disgraceful treatment to our white prisoners in Tabora at the beginning of the war. They were vilely treated and put onto the lowest type of work imaginable – we hear that now they are treating our men very well as they must know it is only a question of a few months now.

DONALD'S DIARY ENDS

(courtesy of the Bundesarchiv)

ZEPPELIN OVER AFRICA

At the beginning of the war there were plenty of rumours of zeppelin attacks. As far-fetched as that might seem, in 1917, the Germans hatched a plan to help the beleaguered von Lettow-Vorbeck. The L59, a custom-built zeppelin, was launched from a German base in Bulgaria. Designed to carry medical supplies and ammunition, it was longer than most zeppelins and manufactured in a manner so that its components could be re-used by von Lettow's troops.

Clumsy and unwieldy, the modified size of the L59 was lacking in power and ballast. She finally took off on 21st November but soon ran into a storm over Crete. The hot air from the desert sands in Libya caused terrible updraughts and one of the engines seized. Cool air over the Nile then stalled her remaining engine and she almost crashed but managed to continue to Sudan. Radio communication was intermittent after the storm damage, but eventually, the crew received a communication via Berlin to turn back. Von Lettow was unable to guarantee he would make the rendezvous as the Allies were on his tail. The British intelligence officer, Richard Meinertzhagen, claimed that the mission had been intercepted by the British, but in fact, Berlin was acting on rumours that von Lettow's army had been overrun. While only some of von Lettow's troops had surrendered on the border of Portuguese East Africa, the trip would have been futile, as the Germans were well over the Rovuma River by the time it would have landed. The L.59 returned to Bulgaria having flown some 4,200 miles.

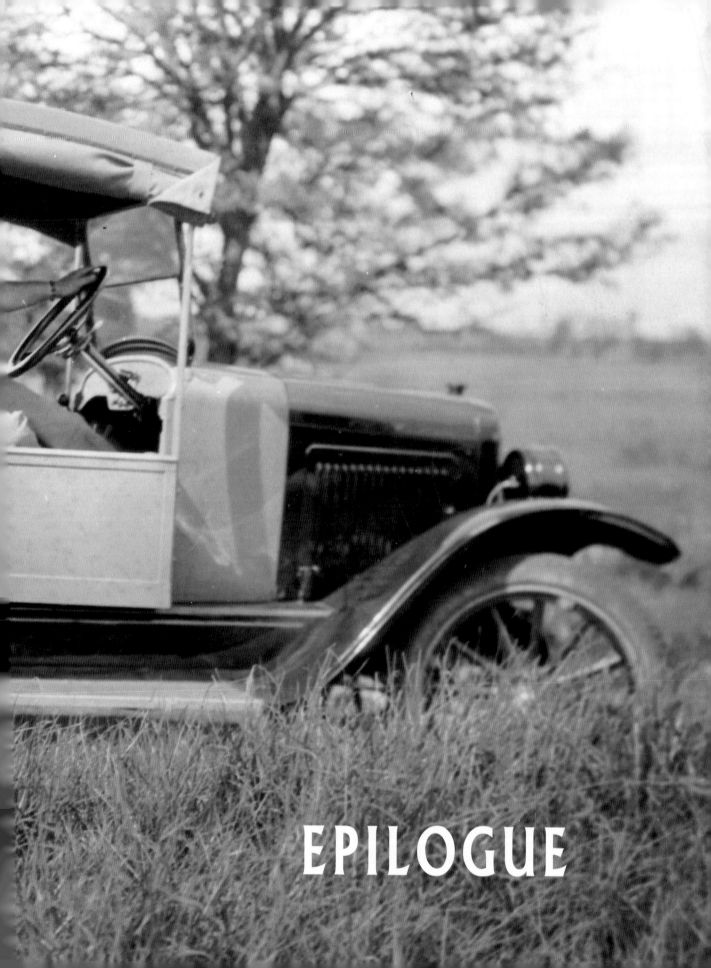

EPILOGUE

A.C. Hoey arriving in Martin's Camp at Nowdoo, circa 1908.

While Donald recuperated in Nairobi, the hunt for the Germans continued deep into the South of German East Africa. With the major towns now under allied control, Smuts considered the campaign to be more of a cleaning up exercise. When he departed to attend the Imperial Conference in London in 1917, command was handed over to General Hoskins and then after Lindi, to General Deventer. "Von Splosh" was a brusque Boer who spoke only Afrikaans and a born-fighter. Grogan who served on his staff regarded him as a "splendid specimen of humanity" and despite the language barrier spent many an evening discussing farming methods. General Northey was reponsible for the final clean-up and his 'Norforce' chased the heels of the Germans into Northern Rhodesia.

Von Lettow's army, greatly reduced in size and weaponry, was driven across the Rovuma into Portuguese East Africa where he managed to capture fresh stocks of supplies and arms. For the rest of the war, Von Lettow played a vicious game of cat and mouse, outwitting the allies at every turn. He even marched back into German East Africa, from Portuguese East Africa and from there entered Northern Rhodesia. He was planning to attack the Belgian copper mines in Katanga when news of Germany's surrender finally reached him. He formally surrendered at Abercorn on 25th November 1918, a good two weeks after armistice had been declared in Europe. His straggling army consisted of thirty officers, 125 European soldiers and 1,165 *askaris*. The Allies had lost 976 officers and 17,650 men. The white soldiers and officers (including the former Governor Schnee who had fought throughout the war) were given a hero's welcome when they finally reached Germany.

With the fighting finally over, the settlers returned to home to find their farms in such disarray that many had to start from scratch. While crops such as sisal had been in great demand, the lucrative coffee beans had been left to rot in the sheds. Mules, horses and oxen had all been taken and there was a dearth of labour. The Africans who had not been conscripted in the carrier corps were now dying in their droves from Spanish flu. Donald recalled walking to the nearest village to recruit more workers and was confronted with men, women and children literally dying on the side of the road.

There were further tragedies. Martin who was invalided back to England in 1918, was on the ship the "Guildford" when it was attacked by a German U boat. Martin's war file, still stored in the National Archives, is filled with his medical notes and anxious letters from his father. According to the records, he was sent back from Kilwa in

1917 with malaria. The medical assessment dispassionately records that he was diagnosed with asphasia that affected his speech. This ties in with the family stories that he was paralysed from a botched spinal injection. A filed telegram refers to his inability to travel back to England without a European valet and a request that he remain under the care of Blayney Percival in Nyeri which suggests that he was reduced to living in a wheelchair.

For such an intrepid sportsman, being condemned to life as an invalid must have been untenable. Martin took his own life in Nyeri on 5th October, 1922. In the register of deaths, it notes that he was of 'unsound mind.' Suicide carried such a stigma that Tony Seth-Smith had no idea how his uncle died until after Donald's death. Oddly Goldfinch and Blayney, and not Donald, were named as the executors of Martin's will. Their father died a few months later and both Martins are commemorated on a plaque in the family church in Bolney.

Donald rarely spoke of his war experience. His daughter, Anne, remembers that much later on, whilst in conversation, he cricked his neck sharply and a piece of shrapnel popped out. No doubt it had become embedded from his close encounter at Kibata. His health never recovered and he was plagued by stomach problems for the rest of his life. He continued to live in the Kenya Colony, hunting and farming. In the 1930s he married Kathleen Bailey, a huntress in her own right and they settled in Njoro near Nakuru. Ill-health forced Donald return to England in the 1950s where he later died in 1958.

BRITISH VIRAGOES: NUNS, NURSES AND MISSIONARIES

It is unsurprising that there is no hint of a woman in Donald's Diary. The Protectorate was considered a 'white man's country.' When Donald arrived in East Africa there were very few single women: those who emigrated generally accompanied their husbands, or were affianced and quickly married in Mombasa, the moment they stepped off the boat. However, in his letter to General Capell, Colonel Grahame's light-hearted comment about his wife becoming a suffragette indicated that the suffrage movement was also gaining momentum in the Protectorate.

By 1914, British East Africa was no longer considered dangerous and off limits for the 'fairer sex.' In her husband's 1911 handbook, Lady Cranworth contributed a chapter entitled 'Hints for a Woman in British East Africa.' Filled with practical information, she advises prospective settler wives to learn cooking, gardening, stable management and the rudiments of farming. There are instructions on how to supervise African servants and what to wear.

She prepares her lady settlers for a life of isolation with bracing advice on how to keep occupied as "Nearly every settler is a busy man, and if, as is almost certain, he is farming, planting or developing property, in some form or another, his whole day is occupied, and when he is not working, he is planning the next step to prosperity. This absorption in his pursuits is, I am told, a feature of all Colonial life…"

Nothing in her hints would have prepared the women for the war years. When the men disappeared to fight, they were put in charge of the farms and properties, sometimes managing their neighbours' farms as well. The female settlers also volunteered as nurses, working in the convalescent homes and hospitals. In his often damning medical report prepared in 1917, Dr Pike writes of a Miss V. Donkin of the East African Medical Services who had been left to run the Kijabe Sanatorium on her own, without any orderlies or visits by the Medical officers in charge. Violet Donkin had trained as a nurse in Britain before settling East Africa in 1908. In 1913, she was recruited to run the Scott Sanatorium, a convalescent home funded by Sir Northrup McMillan. It became a thriving success and Miss Donkin's convalescence in England at the beginning of 1914 (perhaps as a result of the death of her fiancé, Fritz Schindler, another victim of a lion-mauling), was lamented in the local press. During the war, the Scott Sanatorium became a military hospital specialising in dysentery cases. Miss Donkin later married one of her patients, Donald Sharp, a settler-soldier from Laikipia.

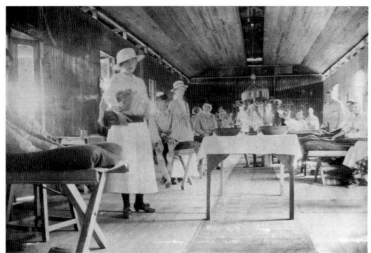

Nurses and patients at the No. 3 British General Hospital where Donald was sent. (courtesy of the Imperial War Museum)

Dr Pike also makes reference to Lady Zelie Colvile and her experiments in creating an emergency ration biscuit for the K.A.R. *askaris.* Lady Zelie Colvile appears to have been an indefatigable matriarch. French by birth, she married Sir Henry Colvile who had fought alongside General Gordon in the relief of Khartoum. Together they had travelled to Madagascar in 1893, stopping off in Mombasa en route where she met Count Teleki and his companion von Hohnel on their return from exploring the Northern Frontier District. It was on this expedition that Teleki discovered and named Lakes Rudolph and Stephanie. The Colviles later moved to Uganda where Sir Henry served as assistant Commissioner of Uganda.

Among Lady Colvile's many achievements (in which cooking could not be included), was as one of few female members of the Royal Geographic Society. After Sir Henry died in 1907, she accompanied her son, Gilbert, to East Africa where he joined Lord Delamere and Galbraith Cole farming livestock in the Rift Valley. In 1914, Lady Colvile opened her Nairobi home to recuperating soldiers. She was disappointed when her nursing home was designated officers only – she found them much more tiresome than 'my dear Tommies.'

Women had also been posted to East Africa by religious institutions. In 1914, the Venerable Sister Irene Stefani had been sent by the Order of Consolata Sisters to work on a mission farm in Nyeri. In August 1916, she joined other missionaries to assist in the military hospital in Voi before travelling to the hospital at Kilwa. Dubbed the 'Angel of Charity' by one British Colonel, she nursed the casualties including many of the African carriers. After the war she returned to British East Africa where she later died after contracting bubonic plague.

Some allied missionaries found themselves on the wrong side of the border when war broke out. Interned at first by the Germans, many were deputed to nurse both German and British casualties in Korogwe, Morogoro and Tabora.

Dr. Norman Jewell recounts meeting Miss Burns who had been imprisoned and later put in charge of a German camp hospital. Robert Dolbey is also full of praise for the 'Angel of Morogoro,' Sister Mabel, who met the Allied army on the entry to Morogoro, carried a letter from von Lettow to General Smuts.

In the Commonwealth War Grave enclosure in Nairobi South Cemetery, an imposing headstone stands apart from the line of white tombstones. It commemorates Leonore Plant of the Kenia Nursing Home. Her epitaph records her death from contracting blood poisoning from one of her patients. There is little information on Leonore apart from a brief mention in the 1917 British Nursing Journal where she is noted as nursing Belgian soldiers in Tabora. It seems that she had come out in 1914 with the Universities Mission, whether she was also imprisoned in German East Africa is unclear.

i) The East African Women's League (still going strong today) was formed in March 1917 as a women only organisation. Among its objectives was the promotion of women's suffrage in the Protectorate. In 1918, after petitioning both the Legislative Council (Legco) and the Secretary of State for the Colonies, it was agreed that white women could be included in proposals for the new electorate. As a result, women in Kenya had the vote before it was allowed in Britain.

ii) In Out in the Midday Sun, Elspeth Huxley describes Lady Colvile as offering to cook invalid dishes for Galbraith Cole: "Lady Colvile turned out not to be a good cook."

iii) The Vatican is in the process of beatifying Sister Irene. One of the miracles she is said to have performed happened long after her death during the war in modern Mozambique. It is alleged that the congregation trapped in a church prayed to her for assistance and the baptismal font filled up with enough water to sustain them.

Askari shooting practice at Lake Baringo, c. 1908.

FOOTNOTES

CHAPTER I

1. Catching the mail seems to be a recurrent theme in Donald's correspondence as the postal service was dependent on the various shipping lines. The Nairobi post office would raise a blue flag when the ship had docked in Aden, a white for its arrival in Mombasa and red to show that the mail had arrived and was ready for collection. It then had to be to be distributed by armed runners. In 1907, Donald described his 'postman' as "very nasty looking," with a headdress, dressed in only a square of a cloth and armed with a long spear.

2. Alan Hawtin Tompson distinguished himself as a scholar and Captain of the First Cricket team at Charterhouse. On graduating from Cambridge, he emigrated to East Africa in 1903 where he soon became a well-respected entrepreneur. Donald relied on him heavily for investment advice and his letters are filled with references to Tompson. He married Gladys Tompson in 1915, just before he left to join the war in France. He was killed at the Battle of Loos. His name is listed on the Memorials at both Muthaiga and Nairobi Club.

3. Conservation in East Africa may seem a modern concept, but there had been discussions over the preservation of its wildlife as early as the 1880s. As the Victorian upper and middle classes became captivated by books such as "King Solomon's Mines" by Rider Haggard and the hunting adventures of R.G. Cummings and Frederick Selous, East Africa became famous as a rich repository of wild animals. Fearful of this new sportsman's paradise becoming like game-depleted Southern Africa (and with some areas already witnessing the reduction in elephant numbers), many hunters and explorers used their 'celebrity status' to express their unease over unregulated hunting. In 1901,

a year after the North and South Game Reserves were demarcated, the Colonial office decided to set up a Game Department. However, there were only funds for a single game ranger. The man who filled the post was the hunter and naturalist, Arthur Blayney Percival, brother to the famous Great White Hunter, Philip Percival. Until Martin's arrival, the department was staffed by a few men, Blayney Percival, R.B. Woosnam, C.J. Ross, George Goldfinch and a small corps of African Scouts.

4. The elder Seth-Smith's diary is pithy but full of dry humour, He describes the aftermath of the stock sales in Nakuru as "hotel bar a wild orgy after the sale - one 'Garland' the leader of the riot said not to be drunk only excited. Would have been called very drunk in England - somewhat amusing to see stout, elderly Dutchman (excited only) dancing to the music of gramophone playing some popular song."

5. The desire for a new club was summed up by Berkeley Cole who said he was tired "of being treated like a pig and that he yearned for a club of a refined nature, where if you wanted a drink, you rang the bell and it was brought to you on a spotless tray."

6. Muthaiga Country Club Magazine, July – September 2018

CHAPTER II

1. German for Country squire and was the name bestowed on the members of the Prussian military who had helped in bringing about German unification.

2. It was one of the von Lettow myths that he had a glass eye. One of the wonderful stories quoted in Edward Paice's "Tip and Run" is that his glass eye was found by an *askari* soldier in the bushes. On returning it to von Lettow, he asked why it had been taken out. Von Lettow replied that he had put it there to make sure the *askari* were doing their duty.

3. The Konigsberg was going to be a thorn in the British side for the duration of the war. Its exploits in the Campaign have been well documented – from sinking the first Merchant ship, the City of Winchester a few weeks after leaving Dar-es-Salaam to destroying HMS Pegasus near Zanzibar. Holed up in the labyrinth of the Rufiji Delta for many months, even when it was destroyed it still caused menace to the British. The Germans cleverly converted the 4.1" guns for use on land. Mounted on giant wheels, each gun was rolled or carried by 400 porters across the difficult terrain. They made their terrifying presence known in many of the battles in the campaign.

4. C.P. Fendall The East African Force 1915 - 1918

5. The Astraea did little damage but realizing that they were a target, Schnee ordered that wireless towers be destroyed.

6. Tom von Prince had been at the Kassel military academy with von Lettow. Half-English he fought in many domestic rebellions in German East Africa, before resigning his commission for a plantation in 1896. He was known as Bwana Sakharani (wild one) and had been instrumental in putting down the Hehe uprising. He died at the Battle of Jasin in 1914. His wife, Marguerite, was rumoured to be the lady sniper in the Taveta Baobab tree.

CHAPTER III

1. It was a difficult decision for neutral nationalities such the Danish Bror Blixen who decided to fight on the Allied side. 'Enemy' citizens were interned and sent to camps in India.

2. As described by Christopher Thornhill in his very readable account "Taking Tanganyika."

3. One of the peculiar events in the history of the war occurred, in 1917, when Germany attempted to send their struggling colonial army a zeppelin with medical supplies. The L.59 was one of the longest zeppelins built and was designed to be dismantled and re-purposed for tents. The L.59 almost made it to East Africa, but over Sudan, received a message to turn back.

4. Edward Paice "Tip & Run."

5. See Appendix for the full letter

KIN

H. BINKS

APPENDICES

APPENDIX I
LETTER FROM DONALD TO HIS FATHER IN 1915

July 30th 1915

My dear Dad,

Very many thanks for your letter of May 30th which reached me on July 27th! I have written Mother and thanked her for the £200 which she is so kindly paying into my a/c.

You ask me how the various properties are doing so I will try and briefly tell you the position of each – We try and muddle on in spite of ¾ of the directors and managers of each concern being away and when in Nairobi I find I have my time more than full seeing to various companies – but I hate in these times of war to be thinking of business at all.

Sisal Ltd. balance sheet for the last 12 months has just come out showing a profit of £1500 (on a called up capital of £7000) after knocking off £1000 for depreciation of machinery and also paying off £1500 worth of overdraft. There is still an overdraft of approx. £9000 and also we have not on the way out all the Maragua factory £4000 and to be paid for – This ought to start work about May 1st.

The Makuyu factory and estate on which the balance sheet is mainly based is producing a steady 50 tons of dried sisal a month – We have sold all this year – and for the rest of the year at an average of £36.10 a ton in London – freights, insurance etc factory to London are approx. £9.10 therefore sisal is worth about £27 at factory. Fifty tons a month = £1350 a month. Expenses of running the whole plantation including depreciation is and ought not exceed £700 a month. Profit of Makuyu factory then from May 1 1915 to May 1 1916 ought to be £7800, which will practically pay off that overdraft of Sisal Ltd.

Now the Maragua plantation (all part of Sisal Ltd. but will be kept separate in future) will not be running before May 1st with the best of luck. It ought in its first 12 months of running make enough to pay off its overdraft and then make similar profits to Makuyu factory.

You will see from this that provided prices are maintained – labour is available etc etc etc etc – the 2 factories ought to make a profit of £10000 - £15000 a year – so that after overdrafts are paid off – a good dividend could be paid on its tiny share capital of 7000 shares of which I hold 1000 – We have of course ½ share in Mumias stock farm which just pay expenses and also still 23,000 acres of land including Kitetu undeveloped. These figures are of course based on the last 6 months running and cannot be expected to be always maintained.

Posho Ltd called up capital of also approx 7000 shares of £1 each. Machinery for this is now ordered and I only hope that Cowan* has it on its way but he is sure to have difficulty with material – Here we are borrowing the machinery money approx £7000 on the security of the land. Factory ought to be up and ready to work May 1st and figure ought to be the same as Maragua and Makuyu factories but expenses will be slightly higher here owing to labour being harder to get and more expensive. It will probably take 2 years that is up to May 1918 to pay off overdraft – after which it ought to make a profit of £5000 a year on a capital of £7000 – Here there are also another 14,000 acres undeveloped for sale! And worth a £1 an acre. I think I have about 1250 shares in this Co. – as I sold 300 at 3 and 31/4 to Alan Tompson and FOB Wilson. You realise this plantation now 650 acres planted is on your old farm – on the Thika where you straddled the log bridge to cross the Thika on to the island! Which performance I did again last week. This place is badly situated for labour and I am rather nervous of it – it is however a much easier plantation to work being level for the trolley lines than Makuyu – Shames Cox is very young as manager and has to be carefully watched – He however consults me before he buys or does a thing and I try and get out there for 2 or 3 days every month. I should like to sell 1/2 my shares in this if I could get say £4 a share for them and pay off my overdraft as you will see I have nearly all my eggs in the sisal basket.

We may have labour troubles – sisal market troubles – shipping troubles or be beaten by the Germans and so be broke to the world but at the moment we are sitting fairly safely on the edge of the volcano.

Ndaruyu farm is in status quo and likely to be – I hate the sight of it – unsaleable – and madness to spend a bean on it at the moment.

Uganda – I have written you about I think. I put £550 into a plantation here with A. Lambut, FOB Wilson, Hunter and 3 others - £5000 capital syndicate here altogether 2 years ago – planting coffee, cocoa and runner on 3 various places – I inspected them all in fact the Syndicate paid for my whole trip to report on them. They are fairly good but not up to our original expectations – may pay 10% end of next year and eventually 15% but never more – would sell these shares at a small profit of £600.

I have also 130 shares in Kuvuvu Co. Ltd. coffee, cocoa, rubber for which I paid 55/- a share!! Paid 10% last year – ditto probably this – ought to pay 25% eventually. Had for a mug here!

Have also 200 £1 share 15/- paid up in Uganda Plantations Ltd. bought at par – ought to get 10% next year – hit by disease. Moderate.

I hold also the following non-dividend paying concerns bought as specs last year and the year before. 1150 £1 shares in Kilindini sites syndicate Ltd. approx. 150 £1 shares in Kilindini Terminal Lands Ltd. – both these Co. hold valuable land on Mombasa island which is a very restricted area – I consider these shares very valuable as Mombasa Island may one of these days be very very valuable – I would not sell these – but of course they are absolutely non-interest bearing.

100 shares bought at par in Betouviy Gold Mine Madagascar. Was once offered £3 a share – but flood has destroyed dam and mill and working is held up for 6 months. Was offered 30/- the other day – non-dividend paying but am told the alluvial gold is wonderfully rich.

250 £1 shares bought at par in Nairobi stock exchange building and plot. Ought to pay 6% next year – simply held up from working owing to war – would sell these at par.

550 £1 shares bought at par 4 years ago in Kinangop Ltd. 15,000 acres grazing land Naivasha – 10 head cattle had to be shifted owing to war consequently all died. Share worth about 30/- and would sell at that.

356 £1 shares bought at par in Amalgamated garages of BEA. Doing very well owing to war but books in awful state owing to clerks at war – Could pay 10% now and ought to pay same next year. Will be complete after war. Shares for sale at par or small profit, a few of these were bonus shares.

Muthaiga plot 4 acres. Bought last year £320 – prices ought not to go down.

Crors estate plot in Indian quarter Nairobi, paid £400 for it 2 years ago. Has not increased in price at the moment but ought to eventually. Would sell to cover myself.

Ruaraka farm 90 acres bought from Alan Tompson in exchange for motor – Posho Ltd. shares etc – freehold 5 miles from Nairobi. Purchase price £900 - £500 has been paid and £400 still to be paid within 5 year at 8% till paid.

Hope after the war to build and live and develop this property – it ought to be very valuable when developed. I have to be in touch of Nairobi nowadays as I am director of nearly all the above companies and take an active part in the management.

You will see from the above that one these days in the dim dim future things ought to be alright with luck – They have all been acquired out of the approx. £3000 you gave me to start with and the £3000 I borrowed from the Bank – I have moreover managed to live and do myself well and rather extravagantly for 9 years. But at the moment you will see my income is absolutely nothing perhaps £50 a year!!!

Enclosed is the report you ask for on Sisal Ltd. Posho Ltd. and my other interests out here and what I expect to do with them. I think it will interest you – But provided that the war is concluded fairly soon and satisfactorily – I still have another 2 years or so before anything solid emanates from them. I must stop now as I have to dash into Nairobi and catch Ronald Tompson who sails tonight. I am also going to pay another call to the Headquarters Staff and see if there is any news as I do so want to get back and do another "bit." My Austin boots have arrived. V. many thanks.

Your ever loving son

Donald

E. W. Cowan is described in Cranworth as a consulting engineer responsible for harnessing the falls at Maragua. This supplied power to both factories and the coffee factory as well as electricity. In the postwar sisal slump the power plant was sold to the lighting company – and saved Sisal Ltd.

LORD CRANWORTH c.1947

Mr. D. Seth Smith: An Appreciation

From Lord Cranworth, K.G., M.C.

NOT long ago there passed away in England, after a long illness, one of Kenya's earliest settlers, in the person of Donald Seth Smith. As Donald was both my partner and one of my oldest friends I hope that I may be permitted to write a word of appreciation of the loss that Kenya has suffered.

Donald came to Kenya in 1906, just down from Oxford where he had obtained a football blue. He joined forces with Alan Tompson, my brother-in-law, Mervyn Ridley and myself and we took up land at Makuyu next door to those splendid pioneers Messrs. Swift and Rutherford, and decided to follow their example and grow sisal, Donald and Mervyn to be the initial managers.

Devoted efforts

We formed a company and that company, Sisal Ltd., has existed and indeed flourished for over 50 years — this mainly through the devoted efforts of its two young managers, who stuck to the long hard task through good times and bad.

I do not think anyone ever acquired a better friend and more loyal partner. Donald was a good business man and most tenacious. Almost his only relaxation was shooting, both with gun and rifles; and in a country of sportsmen I have known no better, with a profound knowledge of bird and beast.

Up till the First World War he stuck to the plantation with hardly a holiday, but when war came he felt constrained to take his part and joined the K.A.R. where, as was to be expected, he became a first-class soldier and was awarded an M.C. for gallantry in the field.

Invaluable help

The war over, he returned to farming having added other enterprises to sisal and though he never sought it, he was always ready to give his services to public work, where his practical common sense was invaluable.

His last years were clouded by illness and I think that after his active life, his enforced idleness irked him. He was always a great lover of Kenya and in these difficult times we can ill afford to lose him.

Now he has passed on and our sympathy must go to his widow, family and many friends.

APPENDIX II
THE GREAT WAR IN
EAST AFRICA
TIME LINE OF SELECTED BATTLES & EVENTS

1914

31 July	Konigsberg leaves Dar-es-Salaam
6 August	Konigsberg captures City of Winchester
9 August	Astrea and Pegasus shell Dar-es-Salaam;
14 August	Hedwig von Wissmann attacks Congo
	German dhow captured on Lake Victoria
5 August	Germans capture Taveta (BEA)
17 August	Troops from Uganda invade Buddu, GEA.
	Pegasus raids Tanga (GEA);
22 August	Germans attack Belgian ship
	Lake Tanganyika
23 August	Royal Naval attempt to land at Bagamoyo
24 August	Germans invade PEA. German attack on
	Abercorn (Northern Rhodesia)
6 September	Fighting in Tsavo Valley (BEA)
9 September	Fighting at Karonga (Nyasa)
11 September	German attack on Mwanza (BEA);
12 September	The fight at Kisii (BEA)
13 September	Kavirondo action on Lake Victoria
14 September	British forces in Uganda advance to
	the Kagera River (GEA)
15 September	Germans leave Mwanza on Lake Victoria
20 September	Konigsberg sinks Pegasus in
	Zanzibar harbour
24 September	Germans seize Belgian island on Lake Kivu
25 September	Baumstark's force attacks British fort at
	Majoreni, near Mombasa.

7 October	Attack on Gazi (BEA)
16 October	Indian Expeditionary Force B sails;
	Portuguese Expeditionary Force arrives.
31 October	IEF B arrives Mombasa.
	Konigsberg found in Rufiji River
2 November	Battle of Tanga.
3 November	Battle of Longido
17 November	EAMR occupy Longido;
20 November	German attack Kifumbiro (Uganda)
28 November	Goliath and Fox attack Da-es-Salaam
25 December	British occupy Jasin

1915

10 January	British occupy Mafia Island
18 January	Germans re-occupy Jasin
March	British beaten at Salaita
15 April	Tighe appointed CiC
22 June	Bukoba signal station destroyed
23 June	Royal Fusiliers occupy Bukoba
6 July	Mersey & Severn attack Konigsberg
11 July	Konigsberg disabled
14 July	Attack on Mbuyuni
7 September	Grogan's speech
8 September	Settlers vote for conscription
20 September	Battle at Longido West
22 November	Smith-Dorrien appointed GOC

6 December	Fight at Lupembe Point, Lake Victoria	20 September	German coastline under British control
23 December	General Sir Horace Smith-Dorrien leaves England	9 October	Action starts north of the Rufiji Delta

1916

21 January	Longido (GEA) captured by British
22 January	Mbuyuni (BEA) captured by British
26 January	Serengeti (GEA) captured by British
5 February	Smuts appointed GOC
12 February	Battle of Salaita Hill
19 February	Smuts arrives in BEA
5 March	Kilimanjaro campaign starts
8 March	The advance beyond Kilimanjaro
11 March	Battle for Latema-Reata Nek, ends 12 March
18 March	Smuts advance on Usambara railway
18 April	South Africans take Kondoa Irangi
19 April	Belgians invade Ruanda
9 May	Battle of Kondoa Irangi
1 June	Belgians invade Urundi
13 June	Battle of Zuganatto Bridge
7 July	Tanga occupied by Royal Navy and Indian Infantry
24 July	Battle at Malangali GEA
15 August	British occupy Bagamoyo
24 August	Mlali
26 August	Morogoro occupied by British
4 September	Battle of Kikarunga Hill (GEA). Dar-es-Salaam occupied
18 September	Belgians occupy Tabora
19 September	Battle for Mgeta River till 24 Sep 1916

1917

1 January	Battle for the Rufiji River crossing lasts to 19 January
20 January	Hoskins becomes CiC
18 April	Fight at Rumbo
23 April	Attack on Yangwani
25 April	Attack on Lutende
18 May	Attack on Schaeffer's Farm
21 May	Wintgens captured at Tabora; Naumann takes over
30 May	Van Deventer becomes CiC
19 July	Battle of Narumgombe
18 September	Narunyu Action, GEA
22 September	The Nigerians at Bweho-Chini
2 October	Naumann surrenders to Cape Corps at Wanyoki
15 October	Battle of Nyangao/Mahiwa
18 October	German attack at Mahiwa
19 October	Fighting at Lukuledi Mission (to 21 Oct 1917)
25 November	Germans cross into PEA
28 Novmber	Tafel surrenders to British forces
11 December	Horace Byatt appointed administrator over GEA
17 December	Lettow-Vorbeck moves his headquarters to Chirumba (Mtarika) in PEA

1918

13 August	Gold Coast Regiment leaves EA
30 August	Battle of Lioma (PEA) to 31 Aug
8 September	Battle near Mahua (last battle in PEA)
11 November	News of Armistice received at Livingstone (Northern Rhodesia)
13 November	Battle of Kasama (Northern Rhodesia); News of Armistice arrives in Kasama at Chambezi
16 November	Lettow-Vorbeck hands in written unconditional surrender; German troops leave for Abercorn
18 November	General WFS Edwards receives German formal submission of surrender in Abercorn
25 November	Formal surrender of German forces
2 December	Germans leave for Kigoma on St George
8 December	Germans arrive at Da-es-Salaam

POEMS FROM THE EAST AFRICA CAMPAIGN

"We're fighting in a bally Zoo,"
The transport driver said;
"And what is more they never puts
The animals to bed.
And none of them is ever really
Tame until they're dead."
"The lion roars about at night
As beastly as a Hun;
The rhino charges from behind
And keeps you on the run;
This is a war in which a man
Ain't safe without a gun."
"This land is just the outer edge,
And what I wish to know
Is- why the Hun should fight so hard
To keep his bally zoo?
Perhaps he knows he is a beast,
And ought to live here too."
Unknown

Men fight in the land,
The Germans and the English.
God alone knows
What business of cattle is theirs,
But Katavi will bring back our men.
Dig, O Bin Makoma, trenches in Tabora:
Others will arrive, the Belgians
Who eat men!
Sukuma Poem from Tanzania Notes & Records
(4th October 1937) translated by J. Koritschoner

PHOTOGRAPHS

Until 1916 when a compact hand-held camera became available, camera equipment was bulky and burdensome. As a result, the photographs saved by Donald and Martin are a rich resource. Cameras were banned by the military and some of the photos in the albums are similar to those in other archives. Perhaps the reason for this similarity was due to authorised photographers, such as Cherry Kearton, sharing their images. The Bundesarchiv in Germany has an extensive repository of images as the German photographer, Walter Dobbertin, was stranded in German East Africa during the war. He documented his experiences travelling with the Schutztruppe.

In addition to the personal collection, images have been used from the following archives:

National Army Museum: pages 34, 100

Imperial War Museum: pages 93, 117, 121, 180, 192

Winchester College: page 47

Bundesarchiv: pages 20, 23, 121, 187

Smathers Library, University of Florida: page 16 from the EAPHA archive

Tom Lawrence private collection: Page 129

SELECT BIBLIOGRAPHY

BOOKS

Ambrose Brown, James, *They fought for King and Kaiser, South Africans in German East Africa 1916*, Ashanti Publishing, 1991

Anderson, Ross, *The Forgotten Front. The East Africa Campaign 1914 – 1918*, The History Press, 2007

Best, Nicholas, *Happy Valley: The Story of the English in Kenya*, Thistle Publishing, 2013

Blixen, Karen, *Out of Africa*, Penguin Books, 1954

Brett-Young, Francis, *Marching on Tanga (with General Smuts in East Africa)*, William Heinemann, Severn Edition 1935

Buchan, John, *The First World War in East Africa 1914 – 1918*, Leonaur, Oakpast Ltd., 2018

Buchanan, A., *Three years of war in East Africa* (dl.wdl.org)

Capell, A.E., *The 2nd Rhodesia Regiment in East Africa*

Chapman, A., *On Safari: Big Game Hunting in British East Africa*, Longmans, Green, 1908

Cranworth, Francis Bertram, *Kenya Chronicles*, MacMillan & Co. Ltd., 1939

Cranworth, Francis Bertram, *Making of a Colony or Sport and Profit in British East Africa*, MacMillan and Co.,1912

Dolbey, Robert Valentine, *Sketches of the East Africa Campaign*, Library of Alexandria, Project Gutenberg ebook, 2003

Dyer, Tony, *Men For All Seasons (and Legendary Ladies)*, Rowland Ward Publications, 2008

Farwell, Byron, *The Great War in Africa 1914 – 1918*, Viking, 1987

Fendall, C.P., *The East African Force 1915 – 1919, The First World War in Colonial Africa*, Leonaur, Oakpast, 2014

Garfield, Brian, *The Meinertzhagen Mystery, The Life and Legend of a Colossal Fraud*, Potomac Books Ltd., 2007

Gaudi, Robert, *African Kaiser, General Paul von Lettow-Vorbeck and the Great War in East Africa*, C. Hurst & Co., 2017

Hemsing, Jan, *Then and Now, Nairobi's Norfolk Hotel*, Sealpoint Publishing, 1979

Herne, Brian, *White Hunters, The Golden Age of African Safaris*, Holt Paperbacks, 2001

Huxley, Elspeth, *Flame Trees of Thika*, Vintage, 2014

Huxley, Elspeth, *Out in the Midday Sun*, Viking, 1987

Huxley, Elspeth, *Nine Faces of Kenya*, Collins Harvell, 1990

Jewell, Norman Parsons, *On Call in Africa in War and Peace, 1910 – 1932*, Gillyflower Publishing, 2016

Lettow-Vorbeck, Paul, *My Reminiscences of East Africa*, Hurst and Blackett Ltd.,

Lyell, Denis L., *Memories of an African Hunter*, from imprint 1923, republished by Pickle Partners Publishing, 2016

Moyse-Bartlett, H., *The King's East African Rifles, A Study in the Military History of East and Central Africa*, 1890-1945, Gale & Polden Ltd, 1956

Nicholls, C.S., *Elspeth Huxley, a Biography*, Harper Collins, 2002

Nicholls, C.S., *Red Strangers, The White Tribe of Kenya*, Timewell Press, 2005

O'Shea, T., *Farming & Planting in British East Africa*, Newland & Tarlton, 1917

Page, Malcolm, *King's African Rifles, A History*, Pen & Sword Military, 2011

Paice, Edward, *Lost Lion of Empire, The Life of 'Cape-to-Cairo' Grogan*, Harper Collins Publishers, 2001

Paice, Edward, *Tip and Run, The Untold Tragedy of the Great War in Africa*, Weidenfeld & Nicholson, 2007

Parker, Tana, *The Seth-Smith Family and Items of Family Interest*, self-publication, 2017

Percival, A.Blayney, *A Game Ranger's Note Book*

Pretorius, P.J., *Jungleman, An Autobiography*, George Harrap and Co., 1947

Ramsay, Anthea, *The Forgotten Pioneer*, Matador Troubador, 2013

Thornhill, Christopher, J., *Taking Tanganyika: Experiences of an Intelligence Officer 1914 – 1918*, Naval & Military Press, 2004

Wheeler, Sara, *Too Close to the Sun, The Audacious Life and Times of Denys Finch Hatton*, Jonathan Cape, 2006

White, Stewart Edward, *African Camp Fires*, Global Grey 2018

Willson, James, *Guerillas of Tsavo*, self-published, 2012

Smith, Wilbur, *Shout at the Devil*, Pan Books, 2012

RESEARCH PAPERS, ARTICLES AND ON-LINE PUBLICATIONS

Brown, Alison M., *Army Chaplains in the First World War*, University of St Andrews, PhD thesis 1996

Fecitt, Harry, *A soldier's burden* www.kaiserscross.com

Harper, Taylor, *Marching Through Hell: The British Soldier in the First World War's East African Campaign*, University of Massachusetts, phd thesis, 1995

Hughes, Lotte, *Moving the Maasai: A Colonial Misadventure*, St Anthony's College University of Oxford, Phd thesis 2002

Kelly, Nora, *In Wildest Africa: The Preservation of Game in Kenya 1895 – 1933*, University of British Columbia, Phd thesis, 1978

Molkentein, Michael, *The Dominion of the Air. The Imperial Dimension of Britain's war in the air, 1914 -1918*

Paice, Edward, *How the Great War Razed East Africa*, African Research Institute

Samson, Anne, *British, South Africa and the East Africa Campaign, 1914 – 1918: The Union comes of age*, Royal Holloway, University of London, Phd thesis 2003

Samson, Anne, *East And Central Africa, The International Encyclopedia of First World War 1914 – 1918 online*

Samson, Anne, *African Women in War: World War 1*, Talk notes for National Army Museum 5th May 2017

Wilson, Sally, *The Mules are Splendid Company: One Man's Experience of WWI Africa*, Librarian and Staff Publications. Paper 26, 2013

ADDITIONAL RECORDS SOURCED FROM:

Tom Lawrence

Great War in East Africa Assocation: gweaa.com

The National Archives: www.nationalarchives.com

www.ancestry.com

www.westernfrontassociation.com

www.oldafricamagazine.com/blog - CS Nicholls

INDEX

compiled by Sarah Seth-Smith